Angular Shopping Store

From Scratch to Successful Payment

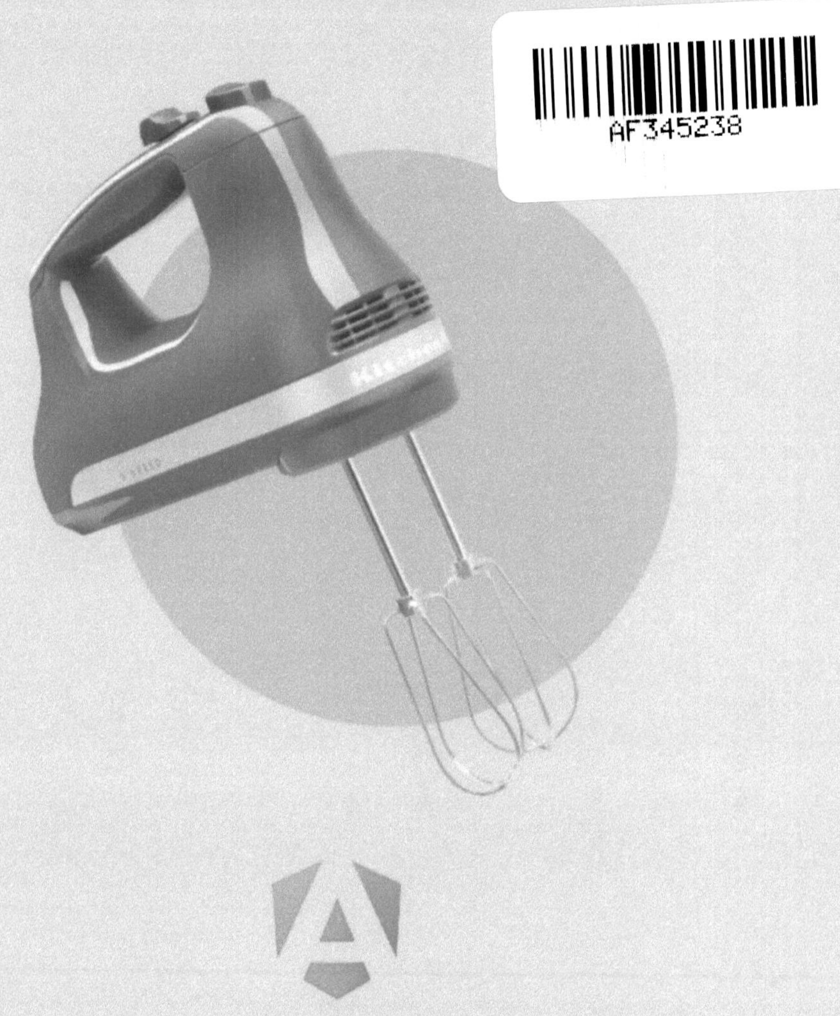

Abdelfattah Ragab

Angular Shopping Store

From Scratch to Successful Payment

Abdelfattah Ragab

Introduction

Welcome to the "Angular Shopping Store".
In this book, I explain how to create an online shopping store using the Angular framework.
To get your store up and running, you need more than Angular.
You need a backend, a database, payment and shipping gateways and much more.
This book is only about the frontend part.
We will create everything from scratch and end up with a complete frontend store.
To make things even more interesting, I have created a small Nodejs application that will help you with Stripe payments so you can sell items in your store.
However, in reality, you need to use webhooks to make sure the money has landed in your Stripe account before you release the product to the customer.
All of these details are part of full-stack development.
In this book, I focus only on the front-end part of the application to strengthen your Angular skills and prepare you for full-stack projects.
By the end of this book, you will be confident working with Angular and ready to work on full-stack projects.
Let us get started.

Source code

The source code is available on the authors' website

https://books.abdelfattah-ragab.com

Chapter 1: Preview

1.1 Desktop Preview

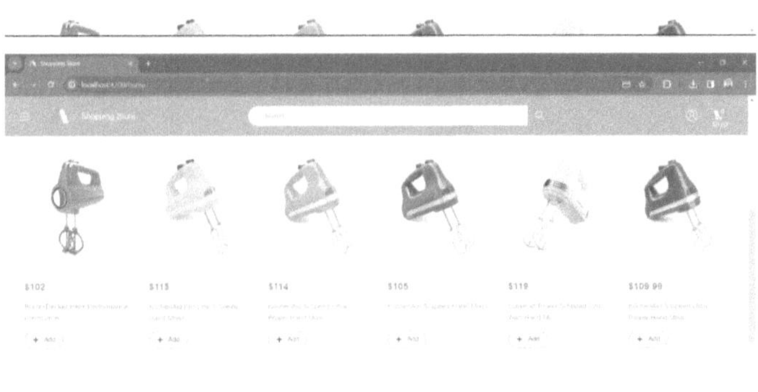

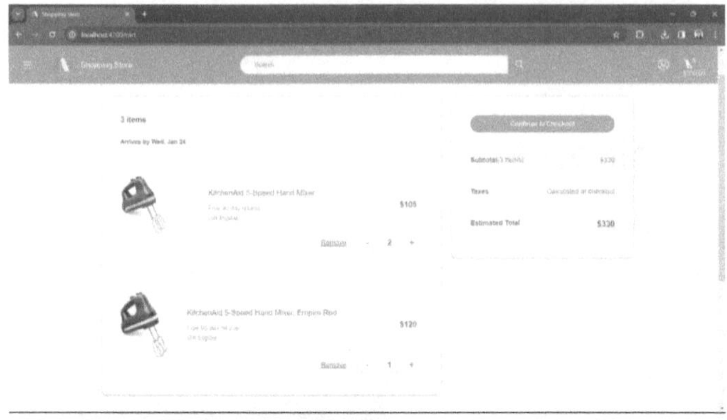
Shopping Store
Search
3 items
Arrives by Wed, Jan 24
KitchenAid 5-Speed Hand Mixer
$105
Remove   -   2   +
KitchenAid 5-Speed Hand Mixer, Empire Red
$120
Remove   -   1   +
Continue to Checkout
Subtotal (3 items) $330
Taxes   Calculated at checkout
Estimated Total $330

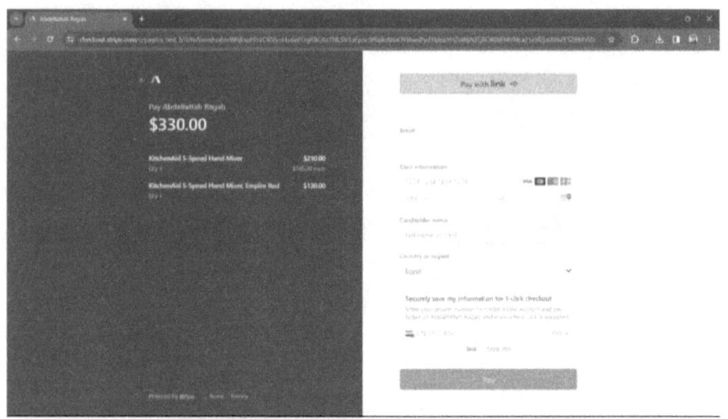
Pay Abdellattah Ragab
$330.00
KitchenAid 5-Speed Hand Mixer $210.00
Qty 2 $105.00 each
KitchenAid 5-Speed Hand Mixer, Empire Red $120.00
Qty 1
Pay with link
Email
Card information
Cardholder name
Country or region
Egypt
Securely save my information for 1-click checkout
Pay

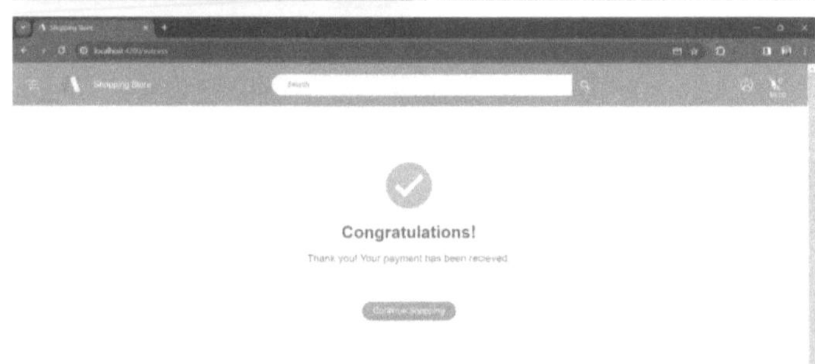
Shopping Store
Search
Congratulations!
Thank you! Your payment has been recieved.
Continue Shopping

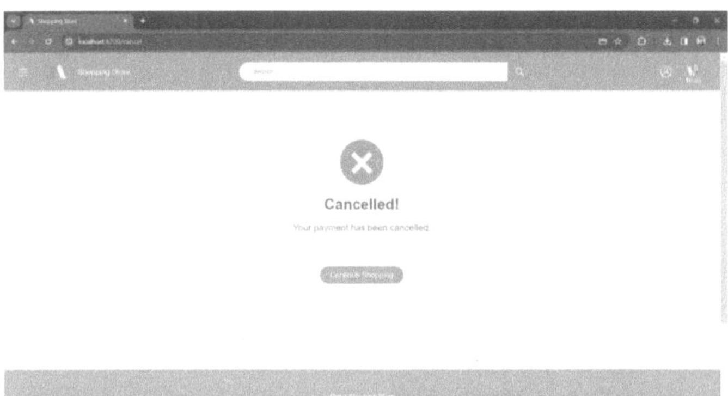
Shopping Store
localhost:4200/cancel
Shopping Store
Search
Cancelled!
Your payment has been cancelled.
Continue Shopping
About Shopping Store

1.2 Mobile Preview

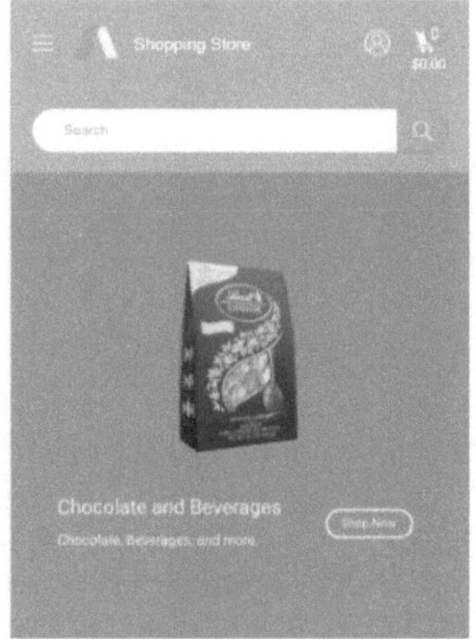

$105

+ Add

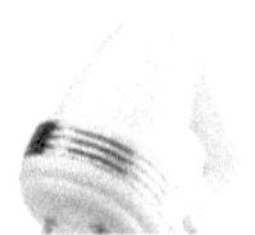

2 items

Arrives by Wed, Jan 24

KitchenAid 5-Speed
Hand Mixer

$105

Remove   -   1   +

KitchenAid 5-Speed
Hand Mixer, Empire
Red

$120

Remove   -   1   +

Continue to Checkout

Continue to Checkout

Subtotal (2 items) $225

Taxes   Calculated at checkout

Estimated Total $225

Email

Card information

1234 1234 1234 1234

MM / YY   CVC

Cardholder name

Full name on card

Country or region

Egypt   ∨

Securely save my information for 1-click checkout
Enter your phone number to create a Link account and pay
faster on Abdelfattah Ragab and everywhere Link is accepted.

010 01234567

link   More info

Congratulations!

Thank you! Your payment
has been recieved.

Continue Shopping

About Shopping Store

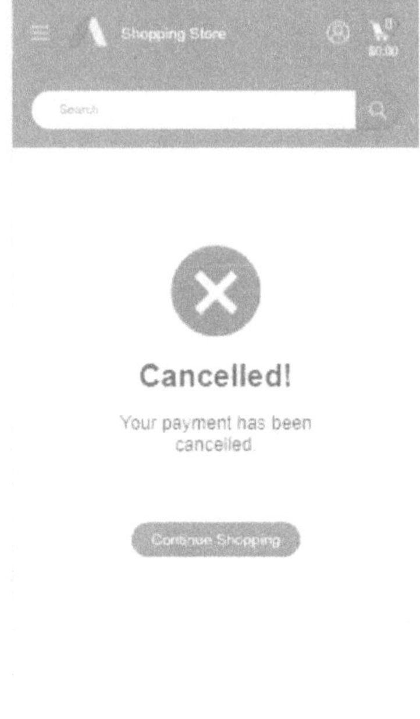

1.3 Application Flow

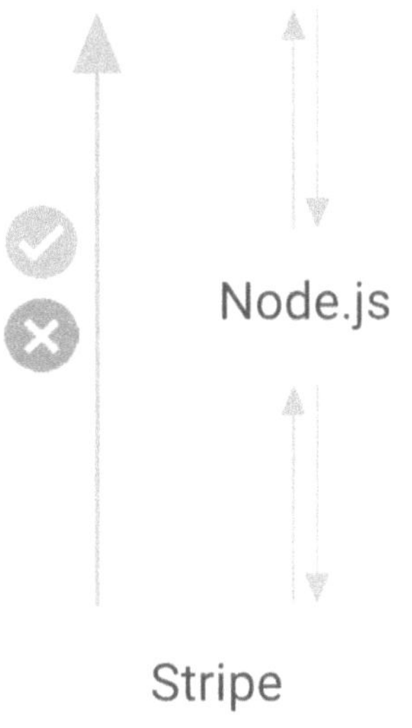

1.4 Projects

- Angular Project
- Node Project

Chapter 2: Angular Project Structure

2.1 Pages

- Home Page
- Cart Page
- Success Page
- Cancel Page

Checkout will be done on Stripe

2.2 Layout

Top Bar

Main Area

Footer

2.3 Home Page Layout

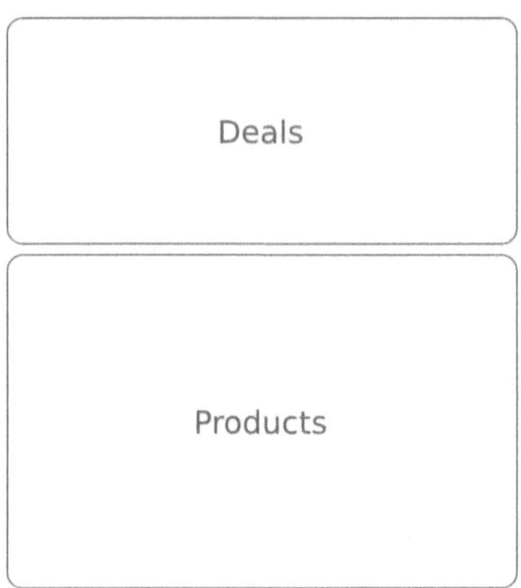

2.4 Cart Page Layout

On desktop

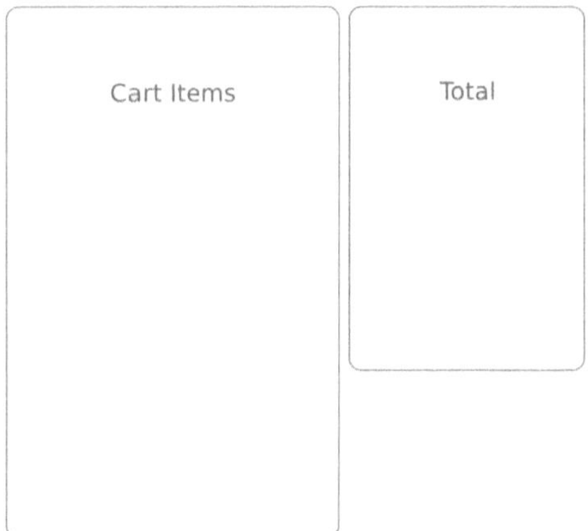

On mobile

Cart Items

Total

2.5 Project Folder Structure

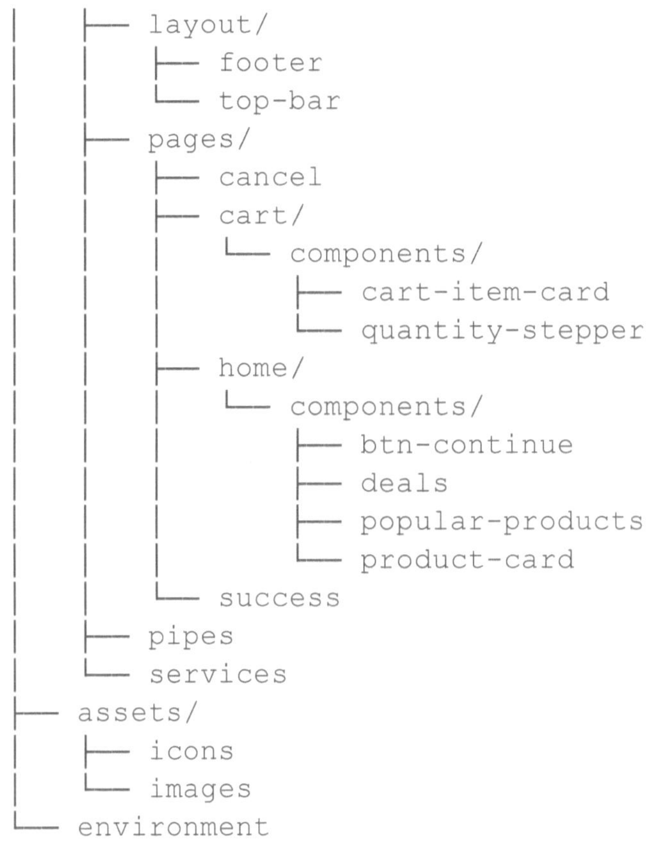

2.6 Development Steps

This is how we will proceed:
1. First I will create the Angular application
2. Next I will create the layout of the application
3. Create the top bar
4. and next Create the footer
5. Create the home page

6. Create the deals component
7. Create the products component
8. Create the product-card component
9. Create the Cart Service
10. Update the products component
11. Update the top bar component
12. Create the Cart Page
13. Create the cart items component
14. Create the cart-item-card component
15. Create the quantity-stepper component
16. Create the total component
17. Create the Node.js application
18. Create the Success page
19. Create the btn-continue component
20. Create the Cancel page

Chapter 3: Create the Angular Application

3.1 Create the Angular Application

Execute the command

```
ng new shopping-store
```

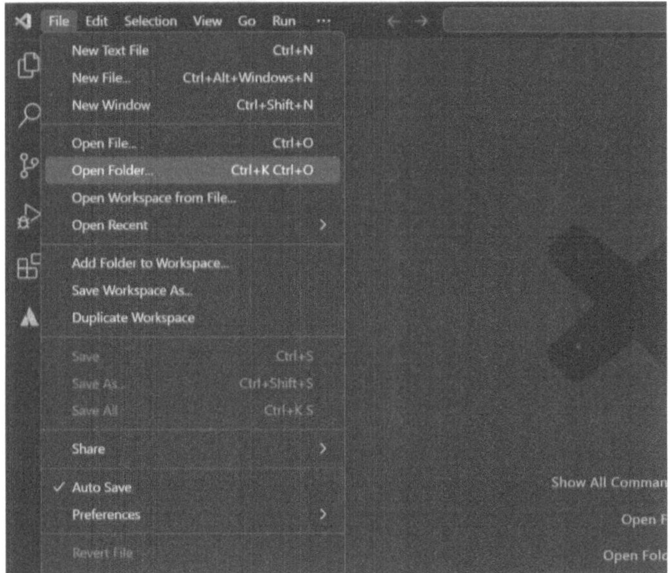

Once done, open the application in Visual Studio Code

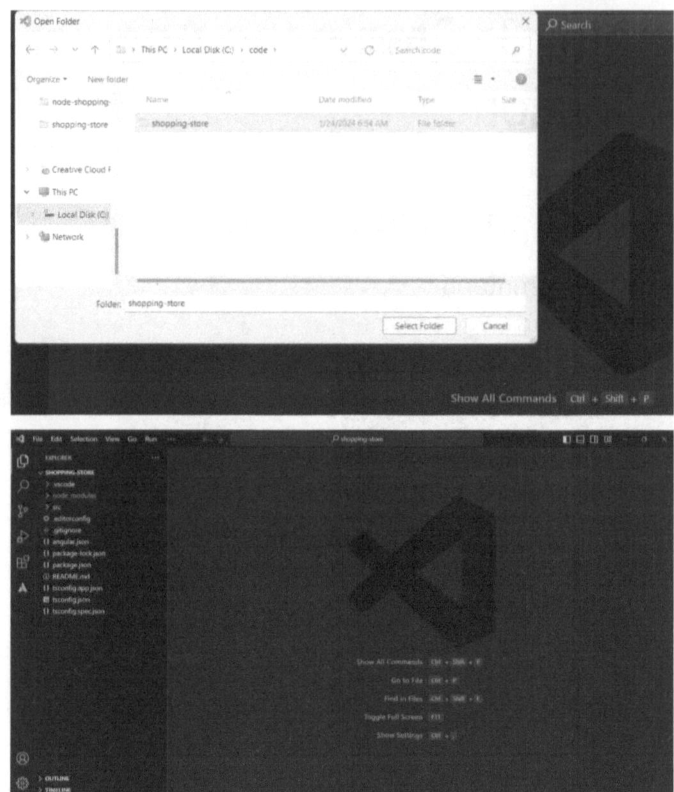

3.2 Preparatory Steps

Copy the assets from the attached project to the assets folder in the new project.

You can download the source code from the book page on the author's website.

Change the application title in the index.html file to "Shopping Store"

```
<title>Shopping Store</title>
```

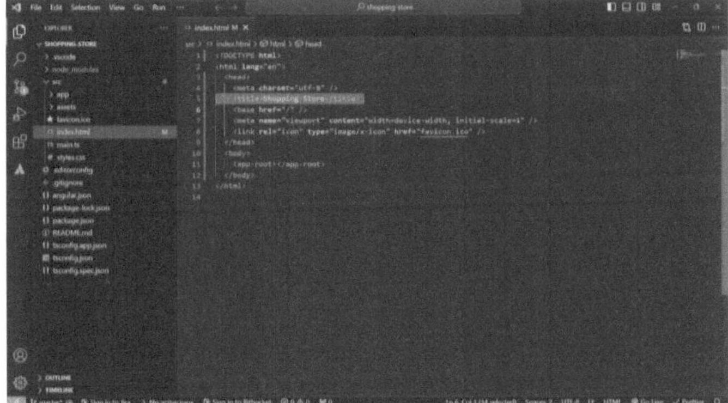

Set the favorite icon of the project to use the logo.png from the images folder

```html
<link rel="icon" type="image/png"
href="assets/images/logo.png">
```

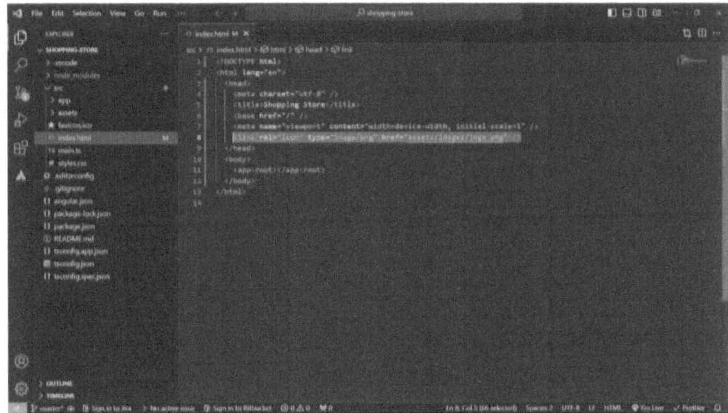

Add the global styles to the styles.css file

```css
* {
  margin: 0px;
  padding: 0px;
  box-sizing: border-box;
```

```css
}
html,
body {
  min-height: 100%;
  background-color: var(--text-color);
  color: rgba(0, 0, 0, 0.7);
}
body {
  font-family: Arial, Helvetica,
sans-serif;
}
.link:hover {
  filter: brightness(1.1);
}
:root {
  --main-color: #2196f3;
  --accent-color: #ff4081;
  --text-color: #ffffff;
  --footer-color: #42a5f5;
  --search-input-height: 40px;
}
.shadow {
  box-shadow: 0 0.0625rem 0.125rem
0.0625rem #00000026;
}
```

3.3 Run the Application

I will first clean up the app component by removing everything and leaving only the last line of the router outlet

```
<router-outlet></router-outlet>
```

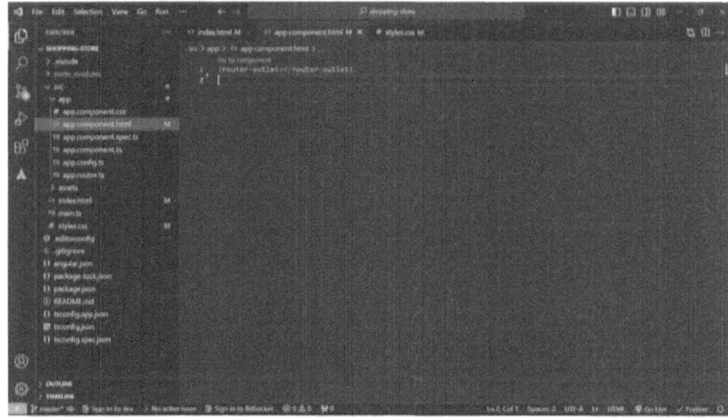

I will also remove the unused favicon.ico

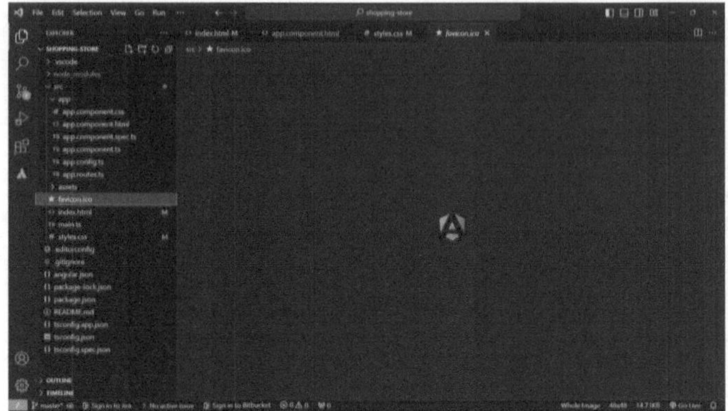

To run the application, open the terminal

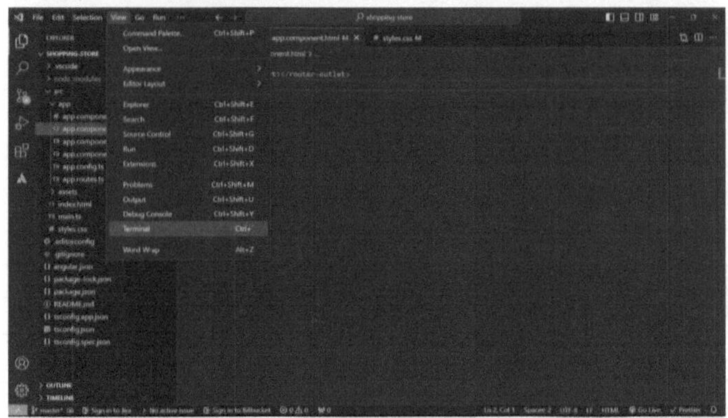

Execute the command

```
ng serve
```

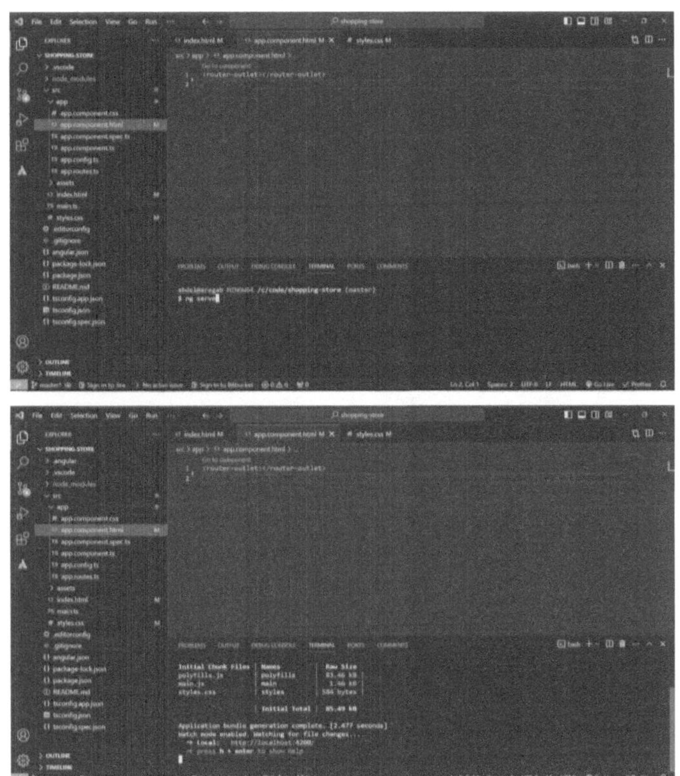

Open the browser to the address http://localhost:4200/

Now I'll start by creating the application layout

Chapter 4: The Top Bar

4.1 Create It

Leave the server terminal open and open a new terminal by clicking on the + in the top right corner of the terminal panel

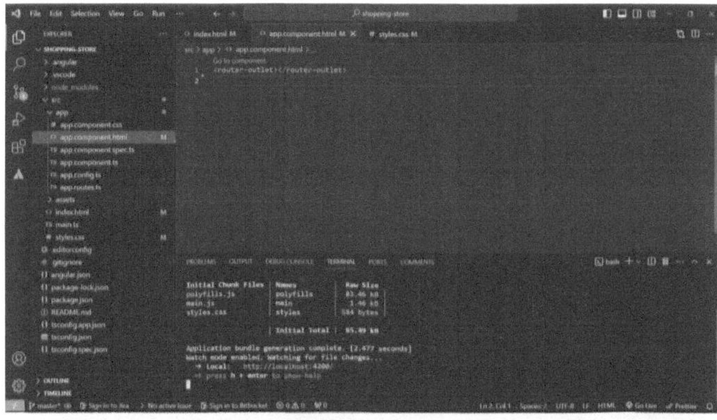

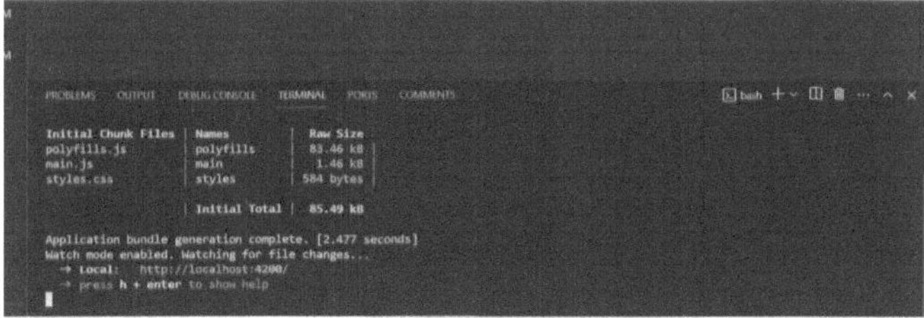

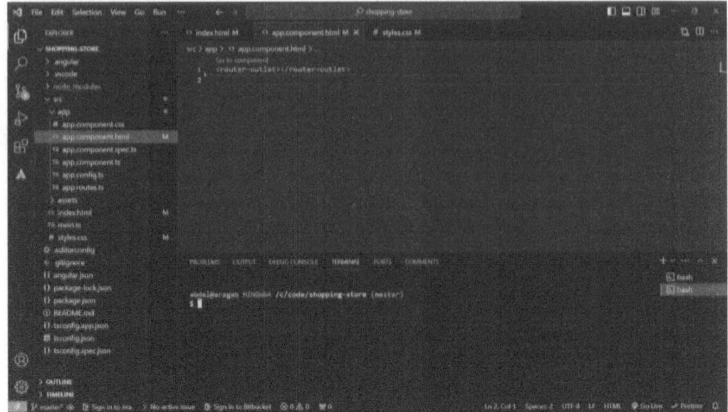

To create a new component using the Angular CLI,
execute the command

```
ng g c layout/top-bar
```

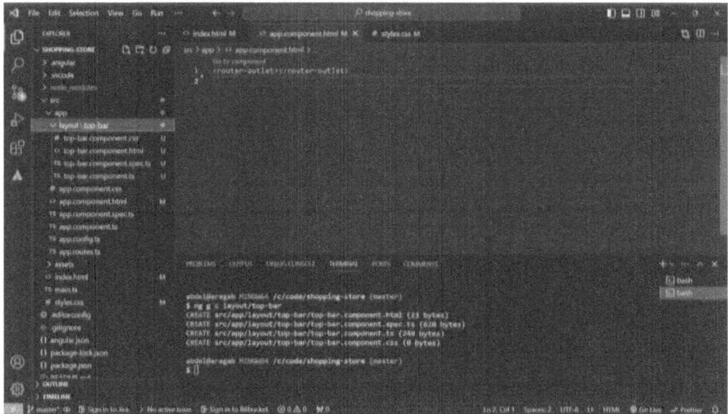

The top bar has three main parts

On mobile it looks like this

For mobiles I will create a second search group in a second line.

So in html we have two search groups, but they should never appear at the same time.

Here is the full code of the component. Throughout the book, I will first introduce the component's TypeScript class, then the HTML code, and finally the CSS code.

4.2 TS

```typescript
import { DecimalPipe } from '@angular/common';
import { Component } from '@angular/core';
import { RouterLink } from '@angular/router';

@Component({
  selector: 'app-top-bar',
  standalone: true,
  imports: [DecimalPipe, RouterLink],
  templateUrl: './top-bar.component.html',
  styleUrl: './top-bar.component.css',
})
export class TopBarComponent {}
```

I am importing the DecimalPipe because I will use the DecimalPipe in the html file to format the currency so that only two decimal places are displayed.
In the html file I will display the values as zeros, but we will change that soon with the numbers from the shopping cart.

Also, the RouterLink is needed to take the user to the homepage when they click on the logo or brand.

4.3 HTML

```html
<div class="wrapper">
  <div class="brand-group"
routerLink="/">
    <img src="assets/icons/menu.png"
alt="" class="menu link" />
    <img src="assets/images/logo.png"
alt="" class="logo link" />
    <div class="brand-name
link">Shopping Store</div>
  </div>
  <div class="search-group">
    <input type="search"
class="search-input"
placeholder="Search" />
    <div class="search-icon-wrapper
link">
      <img src="assets/icons/search.png"
alt="" class="search-icon" />
    </div>
  </div>
  <div class="user-group">
    <img src="assets/icons/user.png"
alt="" class="user-icon link" />
    <div class="cart"
routerLink="/cart">
```

```html
      <img src="assets/icons/cart.png"
alt="" class="cart-icon link" />
      <span class="cart-count">{{ 0
}}</span>
      <span class="cart-total">${{ 0 |
number : "1.2-2" }}</span>
    </div>
  </div>
</div>
<div class="mobile-wrapper">
  <div class="search-group mobile">
    <input type="search"
class="search-input"
placeholder="Search" />
    <div class="search-icon-wrapper
link">
      <img src="assets/icons/search.png"
alt="" class="search-icon" />
    </div>
  </div>
</div>
```

```
1   <div class="wrapper">
2     <div class="brand-group" routerLink="/">
3       <img src="assets/icons/menu.png" alt="" class="menu link" />
4       <img src="assets/images/logo.png" alt="" class="logo link" />
5       <div class="brand-name link">Shopping Store</div>
6     </div>
7     <div class="search-group">
8       <input type="search" class="search-input" placeholder="Search" />
9       <div class="search-icon-wrapper link">
10        <img src="assets/icons/search.png" alt="" class="search-icon" />
11      </div>
12    </div>
13    <div class="user-group">
14      <img src="assets/icons/user.png" alt="" class="user-icon link" />
15      <div class="cart" routerLink="/cart">
16        <img src="assets/icons/cart.png" alt="" class="cart-icon link" />
17        <span class="cart-count">{{ 0 }}</span>
18        <span class="cart-total">${{ 0 | number : "1.2-2" }}</span>
19      </div>
20    </div>
21  </div>
22  <div class="mobile-wrapper">
23    <div class="search-group mobile">
24      <input type="search" class="search-input" placeholder="Search" />
25      <div class="search-icon-wrapper link">
26        <img src="assets/icons/search.png" alt="" class="search-icon" />
27      </div>
28    </div>
29  </div>
30
```

4.4 CSS

```css
.wrapper,
.mobile-wrapper {
  display: flex;
  flex-direction: row;
  justify-content: space-between;
  align-items: center;
  width: 100%;
  height: 80px;
  padding: 10px 20px;
  background-color: var(--main-color);
  color: var(--text-color);
  position: fixed;
  z-index: 100;
  top: 0px;
```

```css
    left: 0px;
    @media (min-width: 760px) {
      padding: 10px 30px;
    }
  }
  .mobile-wrapper {
    top: 80px;
    display: flex;
    @media (min-width: 760px) {
      display: none;
    }
  }
  .brand-group {
    height: 100%;
    display: flex;
    align-items: center;
    gap: 10px;
    @media (min-width: 760px) {
      gap: 20px;
    }
  }
  .menu {
    width: 20px;
    height: 100%;
    object-fit: contain;
    cursor: pointer;
    margin-right: 10px;
    @media (min-width: 760px) {
      margin-right: 20px;
    }
  }
```

```css
.logo {
  width: 42px;
  height: 100%;
  object-fit: contain;
  cursor: pointer;
}
.brand-name {
  text-wrap: nowrap;
  cursor: pointer;
  margin-left: 4px;
  padding: 30px 0px;
}
.user-group {
  display: flex;
  align-items: center;
  height: 100%;
  padding-right: 10px;
  gap: 20px;
  @media (min-width: 760px) {
    gap: 30px;
    padding-right: 20px;
  }
}
.user-icon,
.cart-icon {
  width: 24px;
  height: 100%;
  object-fit: contain;
  cursor: pointer;
}
.cart {
```

```css
    position: relative;
    cursor: pointer;
}
.cart-count {
    background-color: var(--accent-color);
    font-size: 0.9em;
    width: 20px;
    height: 20px;
    border-radius: 50%;
    display: flex;
    text-align: center;
    justify-content: center;
    align-items: center;
    position: absolute;
    top: -4px;
    right: -8px;
}
.cart-total {
    font-size: 0.8em;
    position: absolute;
    bottom: -12px;
    left: 0px;
}
.search-group {
    height: 100%;
    display: none;
    align-items: center;
    @media (min-width: 760px) {
        display: flex;
        margin-left: -40px;
    }
}
```

```css
}
.search-input {
  width: 100%;
  height: var(--search-input-height);
  border-radius: 30px;
  outline: none;
  border: none;
  padding-left: 30px;
  padding-right: 60px;
  @media (min-width: 760px) {
    width: 600px;
  }
}
.search-icon-wrapper {
  background-color: var(--accent-color);
  border-top-right-radius: 30px;
  border-bottom-right-radius: 30px;
  height: var(--search-input-height);
  width: calc(var(--search-input-height)
+ 10px);
  margin-left: calc(-1 *
var(--search-input-height) + 10px);
}
.search-icon {
  width: 100%;
  height: 100%;
  object-fit: contain;
  padding: 11px;
  cursor: pointer;
}
.mobile {
```

```css
    display: flex;
    width: 100%;
    padding-top: 2px;
    @media (min-width: 760px) {
      display: none;
    }
}
```

```css
.wrapper,
.mobile-wrapper {
  display: flex;
  flex-direction: row;
  justify-content: space-between;
  align-items: center;
  width: 100%;
  height: 80px;
  padding: 10px 20px;
  background-color: var(--main-color);
  color: var(--text-color);
  position: fixed;
  z-index: 100;
  top: 0px;
  left: 0px;
  @media (min-width: 760px) {
    padding: 10px 30px;
  }
}
.mobile-wrapper {
  top: 80px;
  display: flex;
  @media (min-width: 760px) {
    display: none;
  }
}
.brand-group {
  height: 100%;
  display: flex;
  align-items: center;
  gap: 10px;
  @media (min-width: 760px) {
    gap: 20px;
  }
}
.menu {
  width: 20px;
  height: 100%;
  object-fit: contain;
  cursor: pointer;
  margin-right: 10px;
  @media (min-width: 760px) {
    margin-right: 20px;
  }
}
.logo {
  width: 42px;
  height: 100%;
  object-fit: contain;
  cursor: pointer;
}
```

```css
52   .brand-name {
53     text-wrap: nowrap;
54     cursor: pointer;
55     margin-left: 4px;
56     padding: 30px 0px;
57   }
58   .user-group {
59     display: flex;
60     align-items: center;
61     height: 100%;
62     padding-right: 10px;
63     gap: 20px;
64     @media (min-width: 760px) {
65       gap: 30px;
66       padding-right: 20px;
67     }
68   }
69   .user-icon,
70   .cart-icon {
71     width: 24px;
72     height: 100%;
73     object-fit: contain;
74     cursor: pointer;
75   }
76   .cart {
77     position: relative;
78     cursor: pointer;
79   }
80   .cart-count {
81     background-color: var(--accent-color);
82     font-size: 0.9em;
83     width: 20px;
84     height: 20px;
85     border-radius: 50%;
86     display: flex;
87     text-align: center;
88     justify-content: center;
89     align-items: center;
90     position: absolute;
91     top: -4px;
92     right: -8px;
93   }
94   .cart-total {
95     font-size: 0.8em;
96     position: absolute;
97     bottom: -12px;
98     left: 0px;
99   }
```

```css
100  .search-group {
101    height: 100%;
102    display: none;
103    align-items: center;
104    @media (min-width: 760px) {
105      display: flex;
106      margin-left: -40px;
107    }
108  }
109  .search-input {
110    width: 100%;
111    height: var(--search-input-height);
112    border-radius: 30px;
113    outline: none;
114    border: none;
115    padding-left: 30px;
116    padding-right: 60px;
117    @media (min-width: 760px) {
118      width: 600px;
119    }
120  }
121  .search-icon-wrapper {
122    background-color: var(--accent-color);
123    border-top-right-radius: 30px;
124    border-bottom-right-radius: 30px;
125    height: var(--search-input-height);
126    width: calc(var(--search-input-height) + 10px);
127    margin-left: calc(-1 * var(--search-input-height) + 10px);
128  }
129  .search-icon {
130    width: 100%;
131    height: 100%;
132    object-fit: contain;
133    padding: 11px;
134    cursor: pointer;
135  }
136  .mobile {
137    display: flex;
138    width: 100%;
139    padding-top: 2px;
140    @media (min-width: 760px) {
141      display: none;
142    }
143  }
```

4.5 Use It

I want the top bar to appear at the top of all pages, so I add it to app.component.html before the router outlet. Open app.component.html and insert the component before the router outlet. However, an error is reported

because app.component does not recognize other components for standalone components.
The first step is therefore to import the TopBarComponent into the AppComponent as follows

```typescript
import { Component } from
'@angular/core';
import { CommonModule } from
'@angular/common';
import { RouterOutlet } from
'@angular/router';
import { TopBarComponent } from
'./layout/top-bar/top-bar.component';

@Component({
  selector: 'app-root',
  standalone: true,
  imports: [CommonModule, RouterOutlet,
TopBarComponent],
  templateUrl: './app.component.html',
  styleUrl: './app.component.css',
})
export class AppComponent {}
```

Now we can use it in the app.component.html as follows

```html
<app-top-bar></app-top-bar>
<router-outlet></router-outlet>
```

```
1   <app-top-bar></app-top-bar>
2   <router-outlet></router-outlet>
```

Go to the browser and it should now look like this

Shopping Store
Search

Congratulations on completing your first component.

4.6 Style the Main Area

In the app.component.html wrap the router-outlet with a "main" css class as follows

```html
<app-top-bar></app-top-bar>
<main class="main">
  <router-outlet></router-outlet>
</main>
<app-footer></app-footer>
```

```html
1  <app-top-bar></app-top-bar>
2  <main class="main">
3    <router-outlet></router-outlet>
4  </main>
5  <app-footer></app-footer>
```

Since the position of the top bar is fixed, it is detached from the normal flow of the document, which means that its height is not added to the overall height of the document.
To replace this, I give the main element a top margin with the same or greater height of the top bar, so that it appears to start after the top bar. I also give it some padding at the bottom.

Add the following styles to the app.component.css

```css
.main {
  height: 100%;
  padding: 160px 0;
  @media (min-width: 760px) {
    padding: 80px 0px;
  }
```

```
}
```

```css
.main {
  height: 100%;
  padding: 160px 0;
  @media (min-width: 760px) {
    padding: 80px 0px;
  }
}
```

Chapter 5: The Footer

5.1 Create It

Execute the command

```
ng g c layout/footer
```

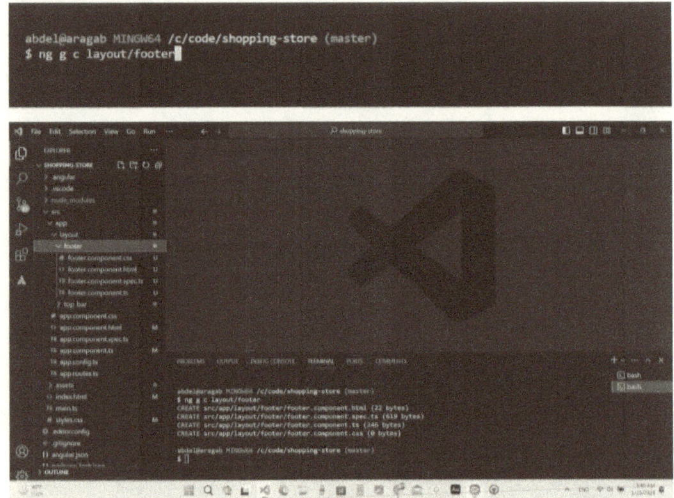

I will display two footers, one for the main links and one for the copyright notice.

5.2 TS

I want to set the year of the copyright notice dynamically, so I define the variable year, which reads the year from the current date

```
import { Component } from
'@angular/core';
```

```typescript
@Component({
  selector: 'app-footer',
  standalone: true,
  imports: [],
  templateUrl:
'./footer.component.html',
  styleUrl: './footer.component.css',
})
export class FooterComponent {
  year = new Date().getFullYear();
}
```

```typescript
import { Component } from '@angular/core';

@Component({
  selector: 'app-footer',
  standalone: true,
  imports: [],
  templateUrl: './footer.component.html',
  styleUrl: './footer.component.css',
})
export class FooterComponent {
  year = new Date().getFullYear();
}
```

5.3 HTML

```html
<footer class="wrapper">
  <div>About Shopping Store</div>
  <div>Help</div>
  <div>Privacy Notice</div>
  <div>Customer Service</div>
  <div>Terms of Use</div>
</footer>
<footer class="wrapper copyright">
```

```
  <p>© {{ year }} Shopping Store. All
Rights Reserved.</p>
</footer>
```

```
1   <footer class="wrapper">
2     <div>About Shopping Store</div>
3     <div>Help</div>
4     <div>Privacy Notice</div>
5     <div>Customer Service</div>
6     <div>Terms of Use</div>
7   </footer>
8   <footer class="wrapper copyright">
9     <p>© {{ year }} Shopping Store. All Rights Reserved.</p>
10  </footer>
11
```

5.4 CSS

```
.wrapper {
    display: flex;
    width: 100%;
    justify-content: flex-start;
    align-items: center;
    flex-direction: column;
    background-color:
var(--footer-color);
    color: var(--text-color);
    padding: 50px 10px;
    gap: 20px;
    font-size: 0.9em;
    cursor: default;
}
.copyright {
    background-color: var(--main-color);
}
```

```css
.wrapper {
  display: flex;
  width: 100%;
  justify-content: flex-start;
  align-items: center;
  flex-direction: column;
  background-color: var(--footer-color);
  color: var(--text-color);
  padding: 50px 10px;
  gap: 20px;
  font-size: 0.9em;
  cursor: default;
}
.copyright {
  background-color: var(--main-color);
}
```

5.5 Use It

Import it in the AppComponent as follows

```ts
import { Component } from
'@angular/core';
import { CommonModule } from
'@angular/common';
import { RouterOutlet } from
'@angular/router';
import { TopBarComponent } from
'./layout/top-bar/top-bar.component';
import { FooterComponent } from
'./layout/footer/footer.component';

@Component({
  selector: 'app-root',
  standalone: true,
  imports: [CommonModule, RouterOutlet,
TopBarComponent, FooterComponent],
  templateUrl: './app.component.html',
  styleUrl: './app.component.css',
```

```
})
export class AppComponent {}
```

```
1   import { Component } from '@angular/core';
2   import { CommonModule } from '@angular/common';
3   import { RouterOutlet } from '@angular/router';
4   import { TopBarComponent } from './layout/top-bar/top-bar.component';
5   import { FooterComponent } from './layout/footer/footer.component';
6
7   @Component({
8     selector: 'app-root',
9     standalone: true,
10    imports: [CommonModule, RouterOutlet, TopBarComponent, FooterComponent],
11    templateUrl: './app.component.html',
12    styleUrl: './app.component.css',
13  })
14  export class AppComponent {}
```

Add it to the app.component.html after the router-outlet as follows

```
<app-top-bar></app-top-bar>
<router-outlet></router-outlet>
```
<app-footer></app-footer>

```
1   <app-top-bar></app-top-bar>
2   <router-outlet></router-outlet>
3   <app-footer></app-footer>
```

In the browser it looks like this

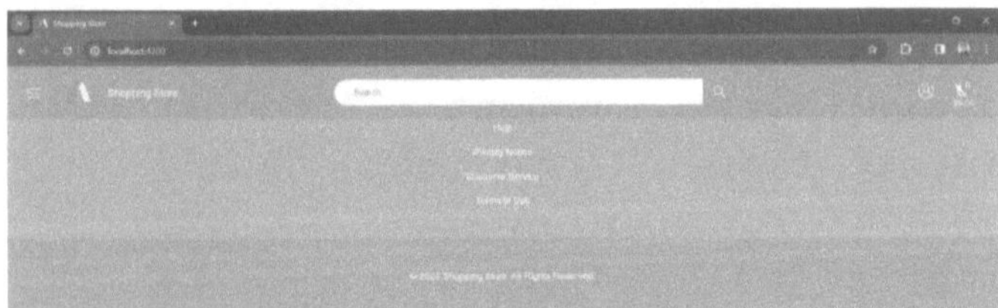

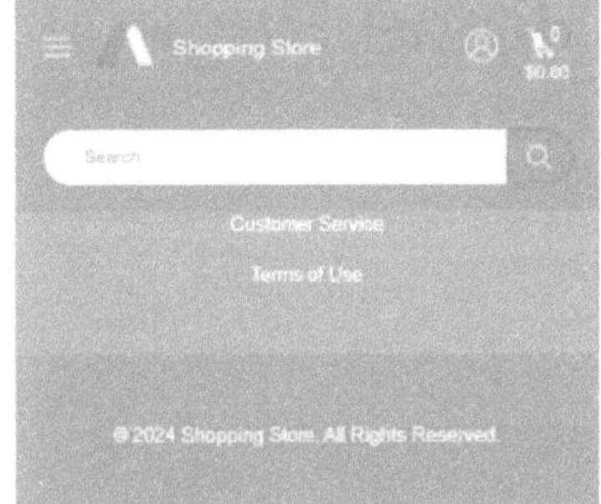

Soon we will add contents.

Chapter 6: The Home Page

6.1 Create It

Execute the command

```
ng g c pages/home
```


6.2 Add Route

Now I will define a new route for the home page and
also set the default route.
Here is the complete code of the app.route.ts

```
import { Routes } from
'@angular/router';
import { HomeComponent } from
'./pages/home/home.component';

export const routes: Routes = [
  { path: '', redirectTo: 'home',
pathMatch: 'full' },
  { path: 'home', component:
HomeComponent },
];
```

```typescript
import { Routes } from '@angular/router';
import { HomeComponent } from './pages/home/home.component';

export const routes: Routes = [
  { path: '', redirectTo: 'home', pathMatch: 'full' },
  { path: 'home', component: HomeComponent },
];
```

Open the application and it should look like this

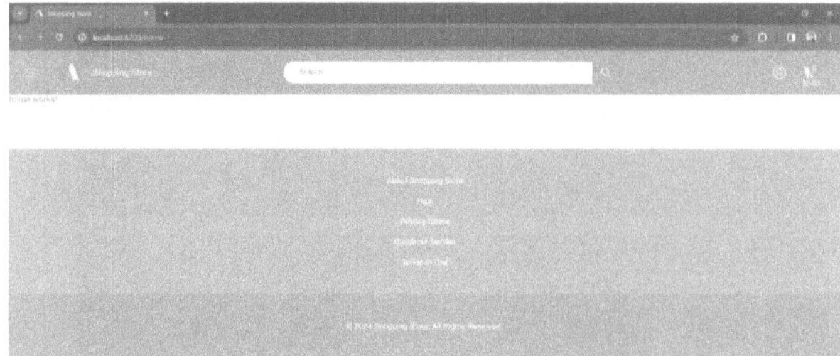

Chapter 7: [Home] Deals

7.1 Create It

Execute the command

```
ng g c pages/home/components/deals
```

7.2 TS

```
import { Component } from
'@angular/core';

@Component({
  selector: 'app-deals',
  standalone: true,
  imports: [],
```

```typescript
  templateUrl: './deals.component.html',
  styleUrl: './deals.component.css',
})
export class DealsComponent {}
```

```typescript
1   import { Component } from '@angular/core';
2
3   @Component({
4     selector: 'app-deals',
5     standalone: true,
6     imports: [],
7     templateUrl: './deals.component.html',
8     styleUrl: './deals.component.css',
9   })
10  export class DealsComponent {}
```

7.3 HTML

For the sake of simplicity, I'll display a picture, but in real life you'll display a carousel instead.
I will use the picture element with two images for mobile and desktop devices.

```html
<picture>
  <source
    class="image"

srcset="assets/images/deals/deal-3-large.jpg"
    media="(min-width: 760px)"
  />
  <img class="image"
src="assets/images/deals/deal-3.jpg"
alt="" />
</picture>
```

```html
<picture>
  <source
    class="image"
    srcset="assets/images/deals/deal-3-large.jpg"
    media="(min-width: 760px)"
  />
  <img class="image" src="assets/images/deals/deal-3.jpg" alt="" />
</picture>
```

7.4 CSS

```css
.image {
  width: 100%;
  height: 100%;
  object-fit: contain;
}
```

```css
.image {
  width: 100%;
  height: 100%;
  object-fit: contain;
}
```

7.5 Use It

Import it in the HomeComponent.ts as follows

```typescript
import { Component } from '@angular/core';
import { DealsComponent } from './components/deals/deals.component';

@Component({
  selector: 'app-home',
  standalone: true,
  imports: [DealsComponent],
  templateUrl: './home.component.html',
  styleUrl: './home.component.css',
```

```
})
export class HomeComponent {}
```

```
1   import { Component } from '@angular/core';
2   import { DealsComponent } from './components/deals/deals.component';
3
4   @Component({
5     selector: 'app-home',
6     standalone: true,
7     imports: [DealsComponent],
8     templateUrl: './home.component.html',
9     styleUrl: './home.component.css',
10  })
11  export class HomeComponent {}
```

Use it in the home.component.html as follows

```
<app-deals></app-deals>
```

```
1   <app-deals></app-deals>
2
```

Open the browser and it will look like this

Chapter 8: Products Data

8.1 Create It

Create a new folder "data" in the "app" directory

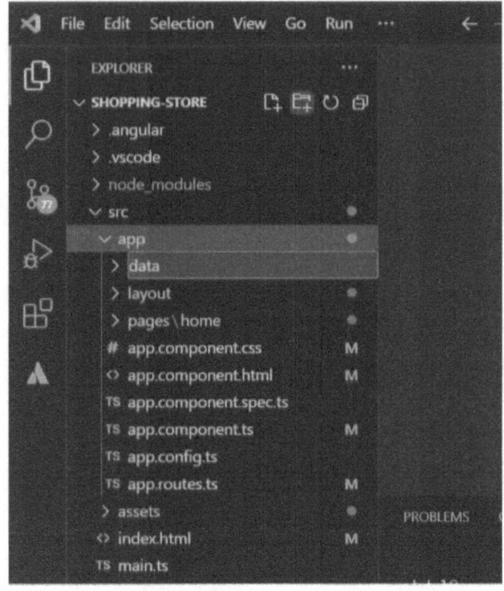

Create a new file "products.data.ts" inside the "data" folder as follows

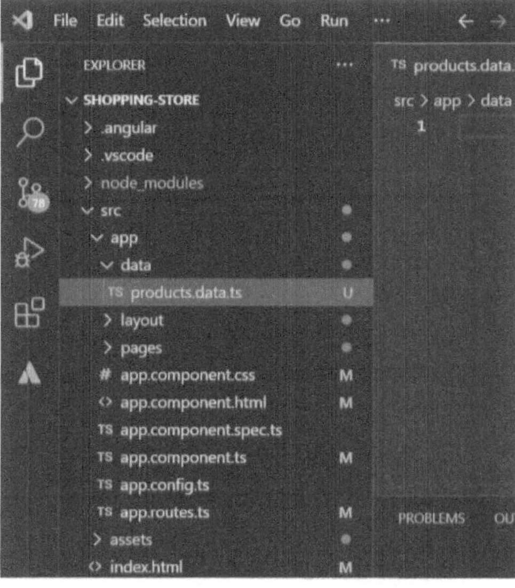

8.2 Product Data Model

Define the Product interface as follows

```
export interface Product {
  id: string;
  name: string;
  price: number;
  thumbUrl: string;
  imageUrl: string;
  description: string;
}
```

```
1  export interface Product {
2    id: string;
3    name: string;
4    price: number;
5    thumbUrl: string;
6    imageUrl: string;
7    description: string;
8  }
```

8.3 Products data

In the same file products.data.ts under the Product interface define the PRODUCTS Data as follows

```
export const PRODUCTS: Product[] = [
  {
    id:
'8347836c-35db-4307-ac5d-cbdf19a9a50c',
    name: 'Black+Decker Helix
Performance Premium Hand Mixer, 5-Speed
Mixer, Red, MX600R',
    description: '',
    price: 102,
    thumbUrl:
```

```
    'assets/images/products/thumbs/8347836c-
35db-4307-ac5d-cbdf19a9a50c.jpg',
      imageUrl:
'assets/images/products/8347836c-35db-43
07-ac5d-cbdf19a9a50c.jpg',
    },
    {
      id:
'f8c2cc34-ddb7-46ec-96ee-e27d1765df10',
      name: 'KitchenAid Pro Line 5 Speed
Hand Mixer, Aqua Sky',
      description: '',
      price: 115,
      thumbUrl:

'assets/images/products/thumbs/f8c2cc34-
ddb7-46ec-96ee-e27d1765df10.jpg',
      imageUrl:
'assets/images/products/f8c2cc34-ddb7-46
ec-96ee-e27d1765df10.jpg',
    },
    {
      id:
'2927b969-1c97-4a36-b4ab-a0777d8690e2',
      name: 'KitchenAid 5-Speed Ultra
Power Hand Mixer',
      description: '',
      price: 114,
      thumbUrl:
```

```
      'assets/images/products/thumbs/2927b969-
1c97-4a36-b4ab-a0777d8690e2.jpg',
    imageUrl:
'assets/images/products/2927b969-1c97-4a
36-b4ab-a0777d8690e2.jpg',
  },
  {
    id:
'57ba7441-8bea-4340-9f49-dc369d108cf7',
    name: 'KitchenAid 5-Speed Hand
Mixer',
    description: '',
    price: 105,
    thumbUrl:

'assets/images/products/thumbs/57ba7441-
8bea-4340-9f49-dc369d108cf7.jpg',
    imageUrl:
'assets/images/products/57ba7441-8bea-43
40-9f49-dc369d108cf7.jpg',
  },
  {
    id:
'552809ab-7ea3-4e48-be23-3c7c53219284',
    name: 'Cuisinart Power 5-Speed
220-Watt Hand Mixer, White',
    description: '',
    price: 119,
    thumbUrl:
```

```
      'assets/images/products/thumbs/552809ab-
7ea3-4e48-be23-3c7c53219284.jpg',
      imageUrl:
'assets/images/products/552809ab-7ea3-4e
48-be23-3c7c53219284.jpg',
    },

    {
      id:
'893deaf7-5224-4702-9ba6-4fc4c52bed22',
      name: 'KitchenAid 5 Speed Ultra
Power Hand Mixer',
      description: '',
      price: 114,
      thumbUrl:

'assets/images/products/thumbs/893deaf7-
5224-4702-9ba6-4fc4c52bed22.jpg',
      imageUrl:
'assets/images/products/893deaf7-5224-47
02-9ba6-4fc4c52bed22.jpg',
    },

    {
      id:
'26917fd7-61c3-41d7-b7cd-3c823bae77d2',
      name: 'KitchenAid 5-Speed Hand
Mixer, Empire Red',
      description: '',
      price: 120,
```

```
    thumbUrl:

'assets/images/products/thumbs/26917fd7-
61c3-41d7-b7cd-3c823bae77d2.jpg',
    imageUrl:
'assets/images/products/26917fd7-61c3-41
d7-b7cd-3c823bae77d2.jpg',
  },
  {
    id:
'30e575f5-8997-4c34-aa44-88af74452db2',
    name: 'Cuisinart 5-Speed Hand Mixer,
Black',
    description: '',
    price: 110,
    thumbUrl:

'assets/images/products/thumbs/30e575f5-
8997-4c34-aa44-88af74452db2.jpg',
    imageUrl:
'assets/images/products/30e575f5-8997-4c
34-aa44-88af74452db2.jpg',
  },
];
```

```typescript
export const PRODUCTS: Product[] = [
  {
    id: '8347836c-35db-4307-ac5d-cbdf19a9a50c',
    name: 'Black+Decker Helix Performance Premium Hand Mixer, 5-Speed Mixer, Red, MX600R',
    description: '',
    price: 102,
    thumbUrl:
      'assets/images/products/thumbs/8347836c-35db-4307-ac5d-cbdf19a9a50c.jpg',
    imageUrl: 'assets/images/products/8347836c-35db-4307-ac5d-cbdf19a9a50c.jpg',
  },
  {
    id: 'f8c2cc34-ddb7-46ec-96ee-e27d1765df10',
    name: 'KitchenAid Pro Line 5 Speed Hand Mixer, Aqua Sky',
    description: '',
    price: 115,
    thumbUrl:
      'assets/images/products/thumbs/f8c2cc34-ddb7-46ec-96ee-e27d1765df10.jpg',
    imageUrl: 'assets/images/products/f8c2cc34-ddb7-46ec-96ee-e27d1765df10.jpg',
  },
  {
    id: '2927b969-1c97-4a36-b4ab-a0777d8690e2',
    name: 'KitchenAid 5-Speed Ultra Power Hand Mixer',
    description: '',
    price: 114,
    thumbUrl:
      'assets/images/products/thumbs/2927b969-1c97-4a36-b4ab-a0777d8690e2.jpg',
    imageUrl: 'assets/images/products/2927b969-1c97-4a36-b4ab-a0777d8690e2.jpg',
  },
  {
    id: '57ba7441-8bea-4340-9f49-dc369d108cf7',
    name: 'KitchenAid 5-Speed Hand Mixer',
    description: '',
    price: 105,
    thumbUrl:
      'assets/images/products/thumbs/57ba7441-8bea-4340-9f49-dc369d108cf7.jpg',
    imageUrl: 'assets/images/products/57ba7441-8bea-4340-9f49-dc369d108cf7.jpg',
  },
  {
    id: '552809ab-7ea3-4e48-be23-3c7c53219284',
    name: 'Cuisinart Power 5-Speed 220-Watt Hand Mixer, White',
    description: '',
    price: 119,
    thumbUrl:
      'assets/images/products/thumbs/552809ab-7ea3-4e48-be23-3c7c53219284.jpg',
    imageUrl: 'assets/images/products/552809ab-7ea3-4e48-be23-3c7c53219284.jpg',
  },
```

```javascript
56
57    {
58      id: '893deaf7-5224-4702-9ba6-4fc4c52bed22',
59      name: 'KitchenAid 5 Speed Ultra Power Hand Mixer',
60      description: '',
61      price: 114,
62      thumbUrl:
63        'assets/images/products/thumbs/893deaf7-5224-4702-9ba6-4fc4c52bed22.jpg',
64      imageUrl: 'assets/images/products/893deaf7-5224-4702-9ba6-4fc4c52bed22.jpg',
65    },
66
67    {
68      id: '26917fd7-61c3-41d7-b7cd-3c823bae77d2',
69      name: 'KitchenAid 5-Speed Hand Mixer, Empire Red',
70      description: '',
71      price: 120,
72      thumbUrl:
73        'assets/images/products/thumbs/26917fd7-61c3-41d7-b7cd-3c823bae77d2.jpg',
74      imageUrl: 'assets/images/products/26917fd7-61c3-41d7-b7cd-3c823bae77d2.jpg',
75    },
76    {
77      id: '30e575f5-8997-4c34-aa44-88af74452db2',
78      name: 'Cuisinart 5-Speed Hand Mixer, Black',
79      description: '',
80      price: 110,
81      thumbUrl:
82        'assets/images/products/thumbs/30e575f5-8997-4c34-aa44-88af74452db2.jpg',
83      imageUrl: 'assets/images/products/30e575f5-8997-4c34-aa44-88af74452db2.jpg',
84    },
85  ];
86
```

Chapter 9: [Home] Products

9.1 Create It

Execute the command

```
ng g c pages/home/components/products
```

9.2 TS

Import the PRODUCTS array into the products variable
as follows

```
import { Component } from
'@angular/core';
import { PRODUCTS } from
'../../../../data/products.data';
```

```typescript
@Component({
  selector: 'app-products',
  standalone: true,
  imports: [],
  templateUrl:
'./products.component.html',
  styleUrl: './products.component.css',
})
export class ProductsComponent {
  products = PRODUCTS;
}
```

```typescript
1   import { Component } from '@angular/core';
2   import { PRODUCTS } from '../../../../data/products.data';
3
4   @Component({
5     selector: 'app-products',
6     standalone: true,
7     imports: [],
8     templateUrl: './products.component.html',
9     styleUrl: './products.component.css',
10  })
11  export class ProductsComponent {
12    products = PRODUCTS;
13  }
```

9.3 HTML

I display the products in a loop. Now I show the product
name, but I'll change that soon and show a product card
instead.

```html
<div class="wrapper">
  @for (product of products; track
product.id) {
  <h3>{{ product.name }}</h3>
  }
</div>
```

```
1  <div class="wrapper">
2    @for (product of products; track product.id) {
3    <h3>{{ product.name }}</h3>
4    }
5  </div>
```

9.4 CSS

```
.wrapper {
  width: 100%;
  display: grid;
  max-height: fit-content;
  grid-template-columns: auto;
  row-gap: 70px;
  @media (min-width: 760px) {
    grid-template-columns: repeat(6,
auto);
    row-gap: 10px;
  }
}
```

```
1   .wrapper {
2     width: 100%;
3     display: grid;
4     max-height: fit-content;
5     grid-template-columns: auto;
6     row-gap: 70px;
7     @media (min-width: 760px) {
8       grid-template-columns: repeat(6, auto);
9       row-gap: 10px;
10    }
11  }
```

9.5 Use It

Import it in the HomeComponent as follows

```
import { Component } from
'@angular/core';
```

```typescript
import { DealsComponent } from './components/deals/deals.component';
import { ProductsComponent } from './components/products/products.component';

@Component({
  selector: 'app-home',
  standalone: true,
  imports: [DealsComponent, ProductsComponent],
  templateUrl: './home.component.html',
  styleUrl: './home.component.css',
})
export class HomeComponent {}
```

```typescript
1  import { Component } from '@angular/core';
2  import { DealsComponent } from './components/deals/deals.component';
3  import { ProductsComponent } from './components/products/products.component';
4
5  @Component({
6    selector: 'app-home',
7    standalone: true,
8    imports: [DealsComponent, ProductsComponent],
9    templateUrl: './home.component.html',
10   styleUrl: './home.component.css',
11 })
12 export class HomeComponent {}
```

Add it to the home.component.html after the deals component as follows

```html
<app-deals></app-deals>
<app-products></app-products>
```

```html
1  <app-deals></app-deals>
2  <app-products></app-products>
```

Open the browser and it will look like this

Search

Black+Decker Helix Performance Premium Hand Mixer, 5-Speed Mixer, Red, MX600R

KitchenAid Pro Line 5 Speed Hand Mixer, Aqua Sky

KitchenAid 5-Speed Ultra Power Hand Mixer

KitchenAid 5-Speed Hand Mixer

Cuisinart Power 5-Speed 220-Watt Hand Mixer, White

KitchenAid 5 Speed Ultra Power Hand Mixer

KitchenAid 5-Speed Hand Mixer, Empire Red

Cuisinart 5-Speed Hand Mixer, Black

Chapter 10: Product Card Component

10.1 Create It

Execute the command

```
ng g c
pages/home/components/product-card
```

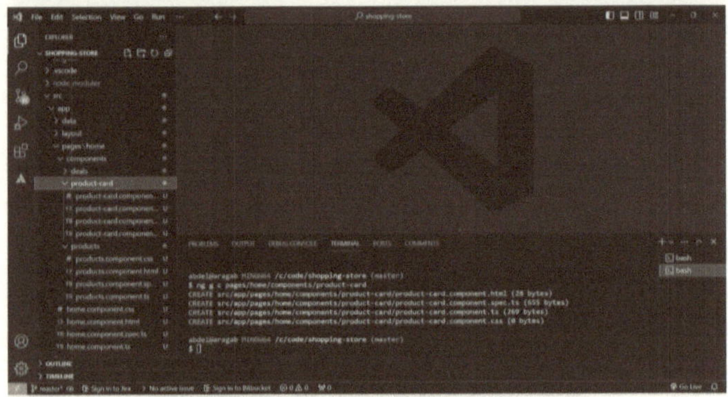

10.2 TS

```
import { Component, EventEmitter, Input,
Output } from '@angular/core';
```

```typescript
import { Product } from
'../../../../data/products.data';

@Component({
  selector: 'app-product-card',
  standalone: true,
  imports: [],
  templateUrl:
'./product-card.component.html',
  styleUrl:
'./product-card.component.css',
})
export class ProductCardComponent {
  @Input() product!: Product;
  @Output() add = new
EventEmitter<Product>();

  onAdd() {
    this.add.next(this.product);
  }
}
```

```typescript
1   import { Component, EventEmitter, Input, Output } from '@angular/core';
2   import { Product } from '../../../../data/products.data';
3
4   @Component({
5     selector: 'app-product-card',
6     standalone: true,
7     imports: [],
8     templateUrl: './product-card.component.html',
9     styleUrl: './product-card.component.css',
10  })
11  export class ProductCardComponent {
12    @Input() product!: Product;
13    @Output() add = new EventEmitter<Product>();
14
15    onAdd() {
16      this.add.next(this.product);
17    }
18  }
```

10.3 HTML

```
@if (product) {
<div class="wrapper">
  <img class="image"
[src]="product.thumbUrl"
[alt]="product.name" />
  <div class="price">${{ product.price
}}</div>
  <div class="name">{{ product.name
}}</div>
  <button class="button link"
(click)="onAdd()"><span>+</span>
Add</button>
</div>
}
```

```
1  @if (product) {
2  <div class="wrapper">
3    <img class="image" [src]="product.thumbUrl" [alt]="product.name" />
4    <div class="price">${{ product.price }}</div>
5    <div class="name">{{ product.name }}</div>
6    <button class="button link" (click)="onAdd()"><span>+</span> Add</button>
7  </div>
8  }
```

10.4 CSS

```
.wrapper {
  background-color: #ffffff;
  height: 500px;
  width: 100%;
  max-width: 600px;
  padding: 20px;
  padding-top: 80px;
  display: grid;
```

```css
  grid-template-rows: 300px 40px 60px
40px;
  border-top: 1px solid rgba(128, 128,
128, 0.5);
  @media (min-width: 760px) {
    border-top: none;
    padding-top: 20px;
  }
}
.image {
  width: 100%;
  height: 100%;
  object-fit: contain;
  cursor: pointer;
}
.price {
  font-weight: 700;
  font-size: 1.2em;
  cursor: pointer;
}
.name {
  width: 100%;
  cursor: pointer;
  font-size: 0.9em;
  line-height: 1.6em;
}
.button {
  outline: none;
  border: 2px solid gray;
  line-height: 1.1em;
  display: flex;
```

```css
  justify-content: center;
  align-items: center;
  gap: 10px;
  width: 80px;
  height: 36px;
  border-radius: 30px;
  cursor: pointer;
  background-color: #ffffff;
  font-weight: 500;
  user-select: none;
}
.button span {
  font-size: 1.8em;
  line-height: 1.1em;
}
.button:hover {
  border: 3px solid rgba(0, 0, 0, 0.8);
}
```

```css
1   .wrapper {
2     background-color: #ffffff;
3     height: 500px;
4     width: 100%;
5     max-width: 600px;
6     padding: 20px;
7     padding-top: 80px;
8     display: grid;
9     grid-template-rows: 300px 40px 60px 40px;
10    border-top: 1px solid rgba(128, 128, 128, 0.5);
11    @media (min-width: 760px) {
12      border-top: none;
13      padding-top: 20px;
14    }
15  }
16  .image {
17    width: 100%;
18    height: 100%;
19    object-fit: contain;
20    cursor: pointer;
21  }
22  .price {
23    font-weight: 700;
24    font-size: 1.2em;
25    cursor: pointer;
26  }
27  .name {
28    width: 100%;
29    cursor: pointer;
30    font-size: 0.9em;
31    line-height: 1.6em;
32  }
33  .button {
34    outline: none;
35    border: 2px solid gray;
36    line-height: 1.1em;
37    display: flex;
38    justify-content: center;
39    align-items: center;
40    gap: 10px;
41    width: 80px;
42    height: 36px;
43    border-radius: 30px;
44    cursor: pointer;
45    background-color: #ffffff;
46    font-weight: 500;
47    user-select: none;
48  }
49  .button span {
50    font-size: 1.8em;
51    line-height: 1.1em;
52  }
53  .button:hover {
54    border: 3px solid rgba(0, 0, 0, 0.8);
55  }
56
```

10.5 Use It

Import it in the ProductComponent as follows
import { Component } from '@angular/core';
import { PRODUCTS } from '../../../../data/products.data';
import { ProductCardComponent } from
'../product-card/product-card.component';

```typescript
@Component({
  selector: 'app-products',
  standalone: true,
  imports: [ProductCardComponent],
  templateUrl: './products.component.html',
  styleUrl: './products.component.css',
})
export class ProductsComponent {
  products = PRODUCTS;
}
```

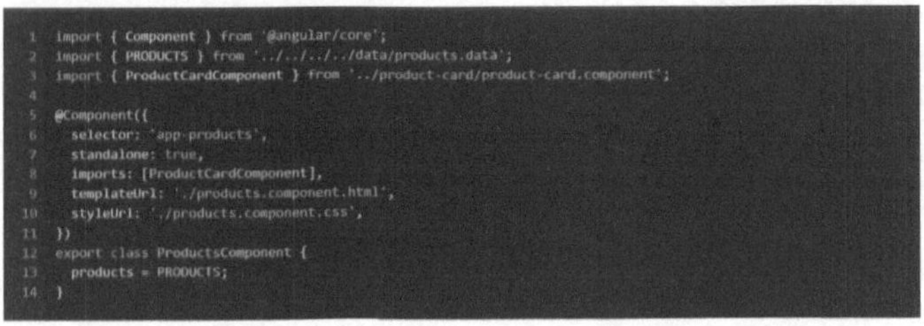

```typescript
1  import { Component } from '@angular/core';
2  import { PRODUCTS } from '../../../../data/products.data';
3  import { ProductCardComponent } from '../product-card/product-card.component';
4
5  @Component({
6    selector: 'app-products',
7    standalone: true,
8    imports: [ProductCardComponent],
9    templateUrl: './products.component.html',
10   styleUrl: './products.component.css',
11  })
12  export class ProductsComponent {
13    products = PRODUCTS;
14  }
```

Now use the new product card to display the products
as follows

```html
<div class="wrapper">
  @for (product of products; track
product.id) {
  <app-product-card
[product]="product"></app-product-card>
  }
</div>
```

```html
1  <div class="wrapper">
2    @for (product of products; track product.id) {
3    <app-product-card [product]="product"></app-product-card>
4    }
5  </div>
```

Update the CSS by adding margin: auto to center it on cell phones, as follows

```
app-product-card {
  margin: auto;
}
```

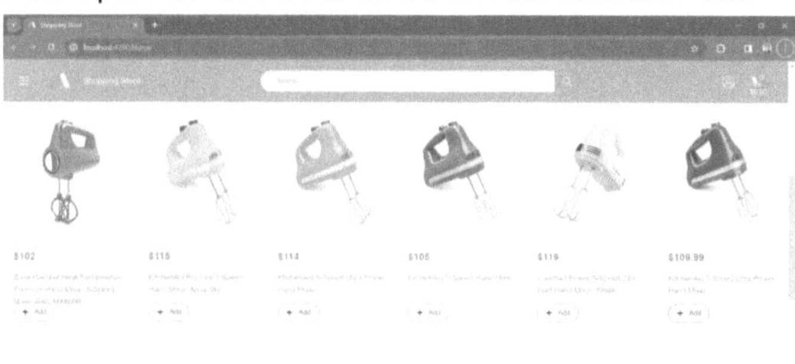

```
12  app-product-card {
13    margin: auto;
14  }
```

Now open the browser and it should look like this

Chapter 11: The Truncate Pipe

11.1 Create It

I will create a truncate pipe to limit the length of the product name.

Execute the command

```
ng g p pipes/truncate
```

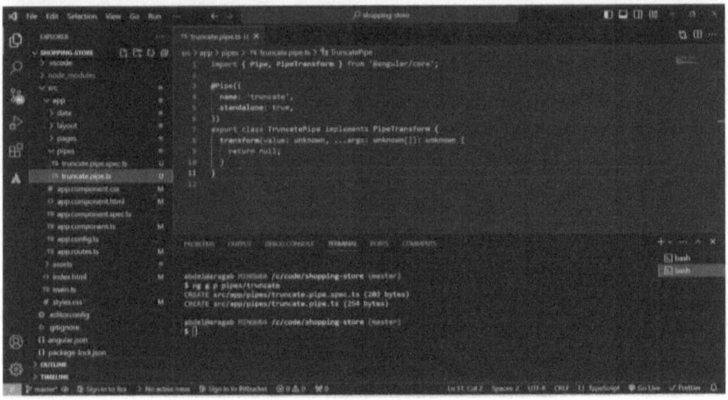

11.2 TS

```
import { Pipe, PipeTransform } from
'@angular/core';

@Pipe({
```

```typescript
  name: 'truncate',
  standalone: true,
})
export class TruncatePipe implements PipeTransform {
  transform(value: string): string {
    const limit = 40;
    const trail = '...';
    return value.length > limit ?
value.substring(0, limit) + trail :
value;
  }
}
```

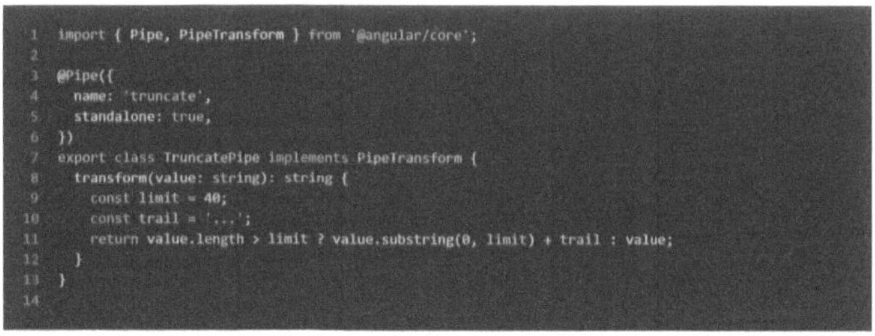

```typescript
import { Pipe, PipeTransform } from '@angular/core';

@Pipe({
  name: 'truncate',
  standalone: true,
})
export class TruncatePipe implements PipeTransform {
  transform(value: string): string {
    const limit = 40;
    const trail = '...';
    return value.length > limit ? value.substring(0, limit) + trail : value;
  }
}
```

11.3 Use It

I want to limit the length of the product name, so I will use it in the product card component.
First import it into the ProductCardComponent as follows

```typescript
import { Component, EventEmitter, Input, Output } from '@angular/core';
import { Product } from
'../../../../data/products.data';
```

```typescript
import { TruncatePipe } from
'../../../../pipes/truncate.pipe';

@Component({
  selector: 'app-product-card',
  standalone: true,
  imports: [TruncatePipe],
  templateUrl:
'./product-card.component.html',
  styleUrl:
'./product-card.component.css',
})
export class ProductCardComponent {
  @Input() product!: Product;
  @Output() add = new
EventEmitter<Product>();

  onAdd() {
    this.add.next(this.product);
  }
}
```

```typescript
1   import { Component, EventEmitter, Input, Output } from '@angular/core';
2   import { Product } from '../../../../data/products.data';
3   import { TruncatePipe } from '../../../../pipes/truncate.pipe';
4
5   @Component({
6     selector: 'app-product-card',
7     standalone: true,
8     imports: [TruncatePipe],
9     templateUrl: './product-card.component.html',
10    styleUrl: './product-card.component.css',
11  })
12  export class ProductCardComponent {
13    @Input() product!: Product;
14    @Output() add = new EventEmitter<Product>();
15
16    onAdd() {
17      this.add.next(this.product);
18    }
19  }
```

Use it in the product-card.component.html as follows

```
@if (product) {
<div class="wrapper">
  <img class="image"
[src]="product.thumbUrl"
[alt]="product.name" />
  <div class="price">${{ product.price
}}</div>
  <div class="name">{{ product.name |
truncate }}</div>
  <button class="button link"
(click)="onAdd()"><span>+</span>
Add</button>
</div>
}
```

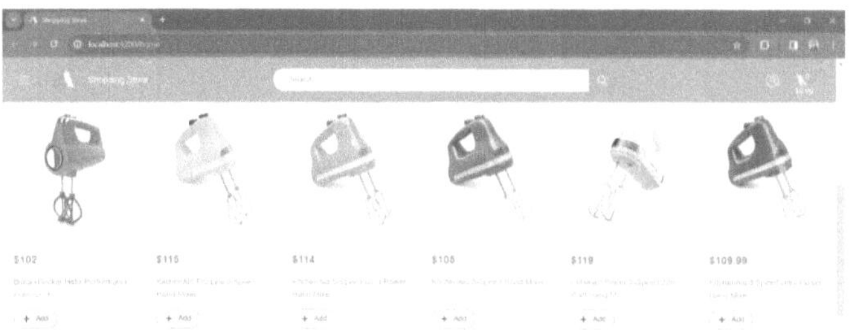

Open the browser and it should look like this

Chapter 12: The Cart Service

12.1 Create It

Execute the command

```
ng g s services/cart
```

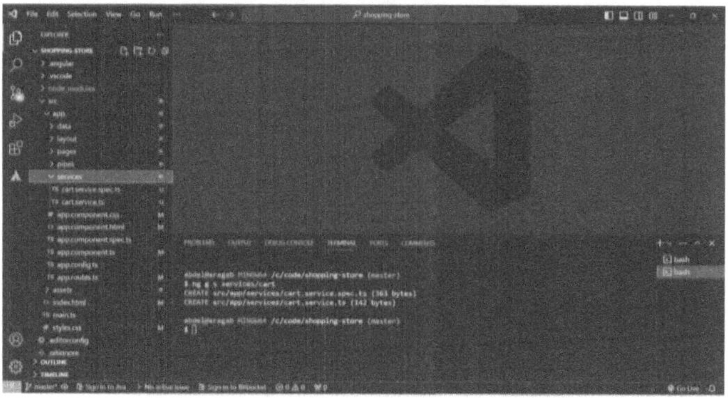

12.2 The Data Models

Define the data models for CartItem and Cart and put them somewhere in the same file before or after the CartService class. I will insert them after the class as follows

```
import { Injectable } from
'@angular/core';
```

```typescript
@Injectable({
  providedIn: 'root',
})
export class CartService {
  constructor() {}
}

export interface CartItem {
  id: string;
  name: string;
  imageUrl: string;
  price: number;
  quantity: number;
}

export interface Cart {
  items: CartItem[];
  count: number;
  total: number;
}
```

```typescript
import { Injectable } from '@angular/core';

@Injectable({{
  providedIn: 'root',
}})
export class CartService {
  constructor() {}
}

export interface CartItem {
  id: string;
  name: string;
  imageUrl: string;
  price: number;
  quantity: number;
}

export interface Cart {
  items: CartItem[];
  count: number;
  total: number;
}
```

12.3 The cart Variable

In the service, declare the cart variable as follows:

```typescript
import { Injectable, signal } from
'@angular/core';

@Injectable({
  providedIn: 'root',
})
export class CartService {
  cart = signal<Cart>({
    items: [],
    count: 0,
    total: 0,
  });
  constructor() {}
}
```

12.4 The addItem Method

Declare the addItem method as follows:

```typescript
addItem(item: CartItem) {
```

```
    const itemObj =
this.cart().items.find((t) => t.id ===
item.id);
    if (itemObj) {
      this.increaseItem(itemObj);
    } else {
      this.cart.update((prevCart) => ({
        ...prevCart,
        items: [...prevCart.items,
item],
        count: prevCart.count + 1,
        total: prevCart.total +
item.price,
      }));
    }
  }
```

```
13  addItem(item: CartItem) {
14    const itemObj = this.cart().items.find((t) => t.id === item.id);
15    if (itemObj) {
16      this.increaseItem(itemObj);
17    } else {
18      this.cart.update((prevCart) => ({
19        ...prevCart,
20        items: [...prevCart.items, item],
21        count: prevCart.count + 1,
22        total: prevCart.total + item.price,
23      }));
24    }
25  }
```

12.5 The increaseItem Method

```
increaseItem(item: CartItem) {
  this.cart.update((prevCart) => {
    const newCart = {
      ...prevCart,
      items: [...prevCart.items],
```

```
    };
    const itemObj =
newCart.items.find((t) => t.id ===
item.id);
    itemObj!.quantity =
itemObj!.quantity + 1;
    newCart.count++;
    newCart.total += itemObj!.price;
    return newCart;
  });
}
```

```
26  increaseItem(item: CartItem) {
27    this.cart.update((prevCart) => {
28      const newCart = {
29        ...prevCart,
30        items: [...prevCart.items],
31      };
32      const itemObj = newCart.items.find((t) => t.id === item.id);
33      itemObj!.quantity = itemObj!.quantity + 1;
34      newCart.count++;
35      newCart.total += itemObj!.price;
36      return newCart;
37    });
38  }
```

12.6 The decreaseItem Method

```
decreaseItem(item: CartItem) {
  this.cart.update((prevCart) => {
    const newCart = {
      ...prevCart,
      items: [...prevCart.items],
    };
    const itemObj =
newCart.items.find((t) => t.id ===
item.id);
```

```
    itemObj!.quantity =
itemObj!.quantity - 1;
    newCart.count--;
    newCart.total -= itemObj!.price;
    return newCart;
  });
}
```

```
39  decreaseItem(item: CartItem) {
40    this.cart.update((prevCart) => {
41      const newCart = {
42        ...prevCart,
43        items: [...prevCart.items],
44      };
45      const itemObj = newCart.items.find((t) => t.id === item.id);
46      itemObj!.quantity = itemObj!.quantity - 1;
47      newCart.count--;
48      newCart.total -= itemObj!.price;
49      return newCart;
50    });
51  }
```

12.7 The removeItem Method

```
removeItem(item: CartItem) {
  this.cart.update((prevCart) => {
    const newCart = {
      ...prevCart,
      items:
[...prevCart.items.filter((t) => t.id
!== item.id)],
    };
    const itemObj =
prevCart.items.find((t) => t.id ===
item.id);
    newCart.count -=
itemObj!.quantity;
```

```
        newCart.total -= itemObj!.price *
itemObj!.quantity;
        return newCart;
      });
  }
```

```ts
52  removeItem(item: CartItem) {
53    this.cart.update((prevCart) => {
54      const newCart = {
55        ...prevCart,
56        items: [...prevCart.items.filter((t) => t.id !== item.id)],
57      };
58      const itemObj = prevCart.items.find((t) => t.id === item.id);
59      newCart.count -= itemObj!.quantity;
60      newCart.total -= itemObj!.price * itemObj!.quantity;
61      return newCart;
62    });
63  }
```

Chapter 13: Use the Cart Service

13.1 The Products Component

Inject the service into the ProductsComponent as follows

```
import { Component } from
'@angular/core';
import { PRODUCTS } from
'../../../../data/products.data';
import { ProductCardComponent } from
'../product-card/product-card.component'
;
import { CartService } from
'../../../../services/cart.service';

@Component({
  selector: 'app-products',
  standalone: true,
  imports: [ProductCardComponent],
  templateUrl:
'./products.component.html',
  styleUrl: './products.component.css',
})
export class ProductsComponent {
  products = PRODUCTS;
```

```
  constructor(private cartService:
CartService) {}
}
```

```
1   import { Component } from '@angular/core';
2   import { PRODUCTS } from '../../../../data/products.data';
3   import { ProductCardComponent } from '../product-card/product-card.component';
4   import { CartService } from '../../../../services/cart.service';
5
6   @Component({
7     selector: 'app-products',
8     standalone: true,
9     imports: [ProductCardComponent],
10    templateUrl: './products.component.html',
11    styleUrl: './products.component.css',
12  })
13  export class ProductsComponent {
14    products = PRODUCTS;
15    constructor(private cartService: CartService) {}
16  }
```

Declare the onAdd method to update the cart and connect it to the product-card component

```
  onAdd(product: Product) {
    this.cartService.addItem({
      id: product.id,
      name: product.name,
      imageUrl: product.imageUrl,
      price: product.price,
      quantity: 1,
    });
  }
```

```
18  onAdd(product: Product) {
19    this.cartService.addItem({
20      id: product.id,
21      name: product.name,
22      imageUrl: product.imageUrl,
23      price: product.price,
24      quantity: 1,
25    });
26  }
```

Pass this to the product-card onAdd event handler as follows

```html
<div class="wrapper">
  @for (product of products; track product.id) {
  <app-product-card
    (add)="onAdd($event)"
    [product]="product"
  ></app-product-card>
  }
</div>
```

```html
<div class="wrapper">
  @for (product of products; track product.id) {
  <app-product-card
    (add)="onAdd($event)"
    [product]="product"
  ></app-product-card>
  }
</div>
```

13.2 The Top Bar Component

Inject the cartService into the TopBarComponent and define two calculated variables for total and count

```typescript
import { DecimalPipe } from
'@angular/common';
import { Component, Inject, computed }
from '@angular/core';
import { RouterLink } from
'@angular/router';
import { CartService } from
'../../services/cart.service';

@Component({
```

```typescript
  selector: 'app-top-bar',
  standalone: true,
  imports: [DecimalPipe, RouterLink],
  templateUrl:
'./top-bar.component.html',
  styleUrl: './top-bar.component.css',
})
export class TopBarComponent {
  total = computed(() =>
this.cartService.cart().total);
  count = computed(() =>
this.cartService.cart().count);
  constructor(private cartService:
CartService) {}
}
```

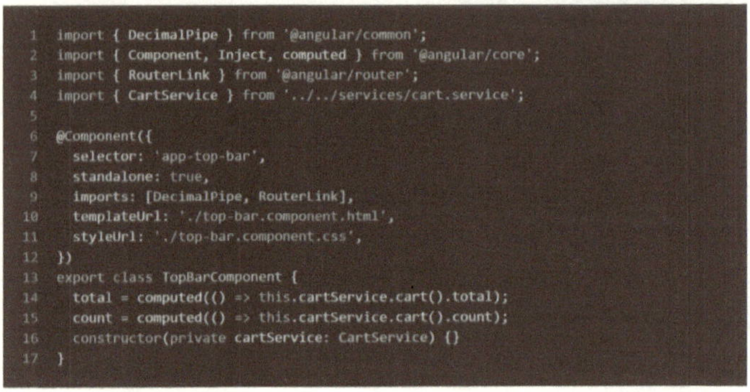

```typescript
1   import { DecimalPipe } from '@angular/common';
2   import { Component, Inject, computed } from '@angular/core';
3   import { RouterLink } from '@angular/router';
4   import { CartService } from '../../services/cart.service';
5
6   @Component({
7     selector: 'app-top-bar',
8     standalone: true,
9     imports: [DecimalPipe, RouterLink],
10    templateUrl: './top-bar.component.html',
11    styleUrl: './top-bar.component.css',
12  })
13  export class TopBarComponent {
14    total = computed(() => this.cartService.cart().total);
15    count = computed(() => this.cartService.cart().count);
16    constructor(private cartService: CartService) {}
17  }
```

Now, replace the zeros in the template by the variables of total and count as follows

```html
<div class="wrapper">
  <div class="brand-group"
routerLink "/">
```

```html
    <img src="assets/icons/menu.png"
alt="" class="menu link" />
    <img src="assets/images/logo.png"
alt="" class="logo link" />
    <div class="brand-name
link">Shopping Store</div>
  </div>
  <div class="search-group">
    <input type="search"
class="search-input"
placeholder="Search" />
    <div class="search-icon-wrapper
link">
      <img src="assets/icons/search.png"
alt="" class="search-icon" />
    </div>
  </div>
  <div class="user-group">
    <img src="assets/icons/user.png"
alt="" class="user-icon link" />
    <div class="cart"
routerLink="/cart">
      <img src="assets/icons/cart.png"
alt="" class="cart-icon link" />
      <span class="cart-count">{{
count() }}</span>
      <span class="cart-total">${{
total() | number : "1.2-2" }}</span>
    </div>
  </div>
</div>
```

```html
<div class="mobile-wrapper">
  <div class="search-group mobile">
    <input type="search" class="search-input" placeholder="Search" />
    <div class="search-icon-wrapper link">
      <img src="assets/icons/search.png" alt="" class="search-icon" />
    </div>
  </div>
</div>
```

```html
1   <div class="wrapper">
2     <div class="brand-group" routerLink="/">
3       <img src="assets/icons/menu.png" alt="" class="menu link" />
4       <img src="assets/images/logo.png" alt="" class="logo link" />
5       <div class="brand-name link">Shopping Store</div>
6     </div>
7     <div class="search-group">
8       <input type="search" class="search-input" placeholder="Search" />
9       <div class="search-icon-wrapper link">
10        <img src="assets/icons/search.png" alt="" class="search-icon" />
11      </div>
12    </div>
13    <div class="user-group">
14      <img src="assets/icons/user.png" alt="" class="user-icon link" />
15      <div class="cart" routerLink="/cart">
16        <img src="assets/icons/cart.png" alt="" class="cart-icon link" />
17        <span class="cart-count">{{ count() }}</span>
18        <span class="cart-total">${{ total() | number : "1.2-2" }}</span>
19      </div>
20    </div>
21  </div>
22  <div class="mobile-wrapper">
23    <div class="search-group mobile">
24      <input type="search" class="search-input" placeholder="Search" />
25      <div class="search-icon-wrapper link">
26        <img src="assets/icons/search.png" alt="" class="search-icon" />
27      </div>
28    </div>
29  </div>
```

Open the application and try to add products

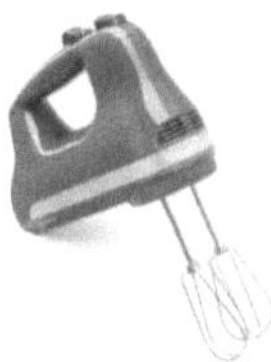

$105

KitchenAid 5-Speed Hand Mixer

$119

Cuisinart Power 5-Speed 220-
Watt Hand Mi

$109.99

KitchenAid 5 Speed Ultra Power
Hand Mixe

Chapter 14: The Cart Page

14.1 Create It

Execute the command

```
ng g c pages/cart
```

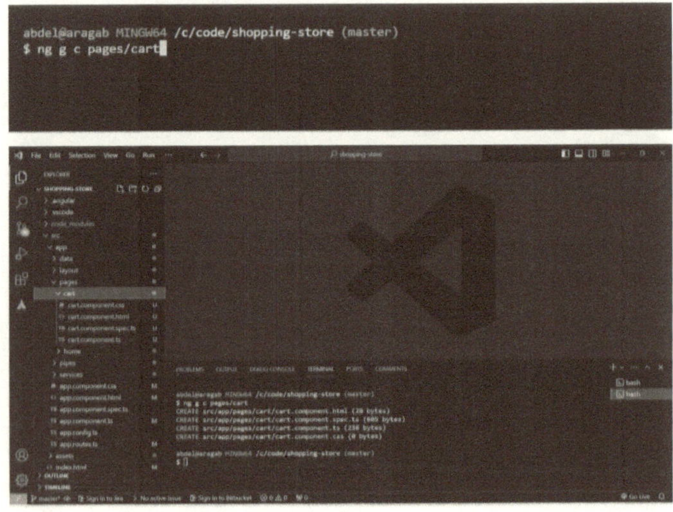

14.2 Add Route

Add a new route for the cart page in the app.route.ts as follows

```
import { Routes } from
'@angular/router';
import { HomeComponent } from
'./pages/home/home.component';
```

```
import { CartComponent } from
'./pages/cart/cart.component';

export const routes: Routes = [
  { path: '', redirectTo: 'home',
pathMatch: 'full' },
  { path: 'home', component:
HomeComponent },
  { path: 'cart', component:
CartComponent },
];
```

```
1   import { Routes } from '@angular/router';
2   import { HomeComponent } from './pages/home/home.component';
3   import { CartComponent } from './pages/cart/cart.component';
4
5   export const routes: Routes = [
6     { path: '', redirectTo: 'home', pathMatch: 'full' },
7     { path: 'home', component: HomeComponent },
8     { path: 'cart', component: CartComponent },
9   ];
```

14.3 TS

Inject the CartService and declare three new variables
for count, total and items as follows

```
import { Component, computed } from
'@angular/core';
import { CartService } from
'../../services/cart.service';

@Component({
  selector: 'app-cart',
  standalone: true,
  imports: [],
```

```typescript
  templateUrl: './cart.component.html',
  styleUrl: './cart.component.css',
})
export class CartComponent {
  count = computed(() =>
this.cartService.cart().count);
  total = computed(() =>
this.cartService.cart().total);
  items = computed(() =>
this.cartService.cart().items);

  constructor(private cartService:
CartService) {}
}
```

```typescript
1   import { Component, computed } from '@angular/core';
2   import { CartService } from '../../services/cart.service';
3
4   @Component({
5     selector: 'app-cart',
6     standalone: true,
7     imports: [],
8     templateUrl: './cart.component.html',
9     styleUrl: './cart.component.css',
10  })
11  export class CartComponent {
12    count = computed(() => this.cartService.cart().count);
13    total = computed(() => this.cartService.cart().total);
14    items = computed(() => this.cartService.cart().items);
15
16    constructor(private cartService: CartService) {}
17  }
```

14.4 HTML

The cart page is organized as follows

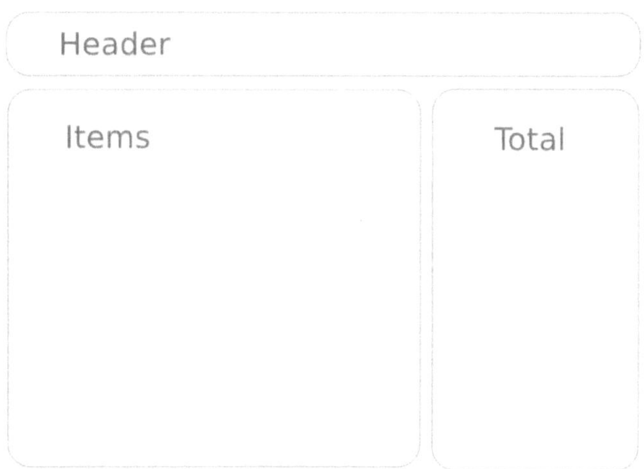

Media queries change the layout for mobile devices as follows

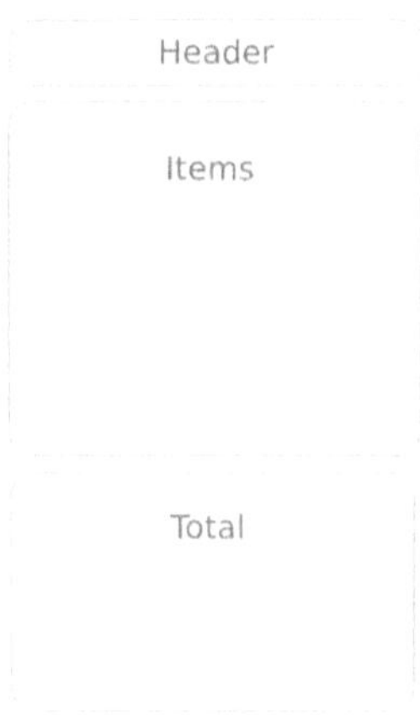

```
<div class="wrapper">
  <header class="header">
    <strong>Cart </strong>({{
```

```html
      count() === 1 ? count() + " item"
: count() + " items"
    }})
  </header>
  @if (count()) {
  <main class="main">
    <div class="items shadow">
      <div class="title">
        <strong>
          {{ count() === 1 ? count() + "
item" : count() + " items" }}
        </strong>
      </div>
      <div class="arrival">
        <strong>Arrives by Wed, Jan
24</strong>
      </div>
      <div class="content">
        @for (item of items(); track
item.id) {
        <h3>{{ item.name }}</h3>
        }
      </div>
    </div>
    <aside class="total shadow">
      <button class="checkout">
        <strong>Continue to
Checkout</strong>
      </button>
      <div class="subtotal value-pair">
        <div>
```

```
        <strong>Subtotal</strong>({{
          count() === 1 ? count() + "
item" : count() + " items"
          }})
        </div>
        <div>${{ total() }}</div>
      </div>
      <div class="taxes value-pair">

<div><strong>Taxes</strong></div>
        <div>Calculated at
checkout</div>
      </div>
      <div class="estimated-total
value-pair">
        <div><strong>Estimated
Total</strong></div>
        <div
class="estimated-total-value">
          <strong>${{ total()
}}</strong>
        </div>
      </div>
    </aside>
  </main>
  } @else {
  <div class="cart-empty">Cart is
Empty!</div>
  }
</div>
```

```html
<div class="wrapper">
  <header class="header">
    <strong>Cart </strong>({{
      count() === 1 ? count() + " item" : count() + " items"
    }})
  </header>
  @if (count()) {
  <main class="main">
    <div class="items shadow">
      <div class="title">
        <strong>
          {{ count() === 1 ? count() + " item" : count() + " items" }}
        </strong>
      </div>
      <div class="arrival">
        <strong>Arrives by Wed, Jan 24</strong>
      </div>
      <div class="content">
        @for (item of items(); track item.id) {
        <h3>{{ item.name }}</h3>
        }
      </div>
    </div>
    <aside class="total shadow">
      <button class="checkout">
        <strong>Continue to Checkout</strong>
      </button>
      <div class="subtotal value-pair">
        <div>
          <strong>Subtotal</strong>({{
            count() === 1 ? count() + " item" : count() + " items"
          }})
        </div>
        <div>${{ total() }}</div>
      </div>
      <div class="taxes value-pair">
        <div><strong>Taxes</strong></div>
        <div>Calculated at checkout</div>
      </div>
      <div class="estimated-total value-pair">
        <div><strong>Estimated Total</strong></div>
        <div class="estimated-total-value">
          <strong>${{ total() }}</strong>
        </div>
      </div>
    </aside>
  </main>
  } @else {
  <div class="cart-empty">Cart is Empty!</div>
  }
</div>
```

14.5 CSS

```css
.wrapper {
  padding: 10px;
  padding-top: 40px;
  @media (min-width: 760px) {
    padding: 0px 200px;
    padding-top: 40px;
  }
```

```css
}
.cart-empty {
  width: 100%;
  display: flex;
  align-items: center;
  justify-content: center;
  text-align: center;
  padding: 80px;
}
.header {
  font-size: 1.4em;
  cursor: default;
}
.main {
  width: 100%;
  display: grid;
  grid-template-columns: auto;
  gap: 20px;
  padding: 40px 0px;
  cursor: default;
  @media (min-width: 760px) {
    grid-template-columns: 65% 35%;
  }
}
.items {
  display: grid;
  grid-template-columns: auto;
  border: 1px solid rgba(128, 128, 128,
0.3);
  border-radius: 10px;
  padding: 40px;
```

```css
}
.title {
  padding-bottom: 0px;
}
.arrival {
  font-size: 0.8em;
  padding-top: 30px;
  padding-bottom: 20px;
}
.content {
  display: grid;
  grid-template-columns: auto;
  row-gap: 40px;
}
.total {
  display: grid;
  grid-template-columns: auto;
  gap: 10px;
  border: 1px solid rgba(128, 128, 128,
0.3);
  border-radius: 10px;
  padding: 40px;
  height: fit-content;
}
.checkout {
  width: 100%;
  color: #ffffff;
  background-color: var(--accent-color);
  height: 36px;
  border-radius: 30px;
  cursor: pointer;
```

```css
  outline: none;
  border: 1px solid gray;
}
.checkout:hover {
  filter: brightness(1.1);
}
.value-pair {
  display: flex;
  justify-content: space-between;
}
.subtotal,
.taxes,
.estimated-total {
  font-size: 0.9em;
  padding: 20px 0px;
}
.subtotal {
  padding-top: 40px;
}
.estimated-total-value {
  font-size: 1.2em;
}
```

```css
.wrapper {
  padding: 10px;
  padding-top: 40px;
  @media (min-width: 760px) {
    padding: 0px 200px;
    padding-top: 40px;
  }
}
.cart-empty {
  width: 100%;
  display: flex;
  align-items: center;
  justify-content: center;
  text-align: center;
  padding: 80px;
}
.header {
  font-size: 1.4em;
  cursor: default;
}
.main {
  width: 100%;
  display: grid;
  grid-template-columns: auto;
  gap: 20px;
  padding: 40px 0px;
  cursor: default;
  @media (min-width: 760px) {
    grid-template-columns: 65% 35%;
  }
}
.items {
  display: grid;
  grid-template-columns: auto;
  border: 1px solid rgba(128, 128, 128, 0.3);
  border-radius: 10px;
  padding: 40px;
}
.title {
  padding-bottom: 0px;
}
.arrival {
  font-size: 0.8em;
  padding-top: 30px;
  padding-bottom: 20px;
}
```

```css
47  .content {
48    display: grid;
49    grid-template-columns: auto;
50    row-gap: 40px;
51  }
52  .total {
53    display: grid;
54    grid-template-columns: auto;
55    gap: 10px;
56    border: 1px solid rgba(128, 128, 128, 0.3);
57    border-radius: 10px;
58    padding: 40px;
59    height: fit-content;
60  }
61  .checkout {
62    width: 100%;
63    color: #ffffff;
64    background-color: var(--accent-color);
65    height: 36px;
66    border-radius: 30px;
67    cursor: pointer;
68    outline: none;
69    border: 1px solid gray;
70  }
71  .checkout:hover {
72    filter: brightness(1.1);
73  }
74  .value-pair {
75    display: flex;
76    justify-content: space-between;
77  }
78  .subtotal,
79  .taxes,
80  .estimated-total {
81    font-size: 0.9em;
82    padding: 20px 0px;
83  }
84  .subtotal {
85    padding-top: 40px;
86  }
87  .estimated-total-value {
88    font-size: 1.2em;
89  }
```

Open the browser and it will look like this

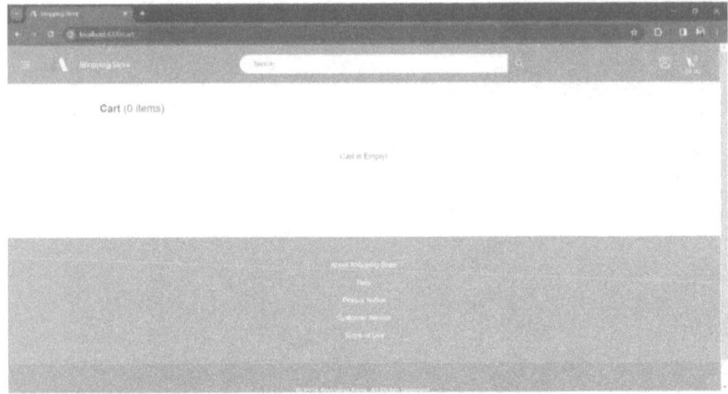

Add some items and it will look like this

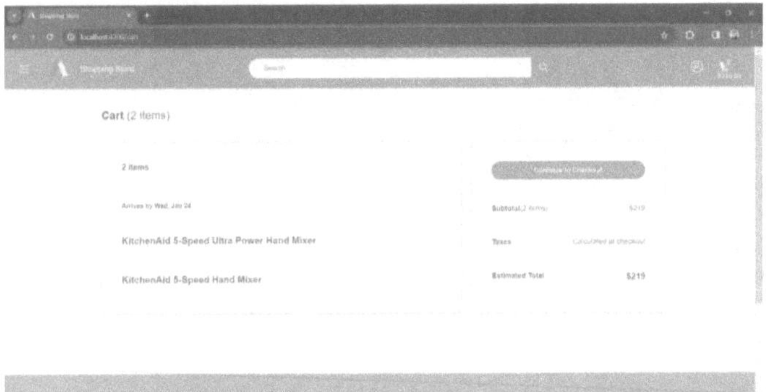

14.6 Scroll Position Restoration

As you can see, the viewport stays down when you navigate over the components.
Let's configure the router so that it scrolls up when navigating
Update the app.config.ts as follows

```typescript
import { ApplicationConfig } from
'@angular/core';
import {
  InMemoryScrollingFeature,
  InMemoryScrollingOptions,
  provideRouter,
  withInMemoryScrolling,
} from '@angular/router';

import { routes } from './app.routes';

const scrollConfig:
InMemoryScrollingOptions = {
  scrollPositionRestoration: 'top',
  anchorScrolling: 'enabled',
};
const inMemoryScrollingFeature:
InMemoryScrollingFeature =
  withInMemoryScrolling(scrollConfig);

export const appConfig:
ApplicationConfig = {
  providers: [provideRouter(routes,
inMemoryScrollingFeature)],
};
```

```typescript
import { ApplicationConfig } from '@angular/core';
import {
  InMemoryScrollingFeature,
  InMemoryScrollingOptions,
  provideRouter,
  withInMemoryScrolling,
} from '@angular/router';

import { routes } from './app.routes';

const scrollConfig: InMemoryScrollingOptions = {
  scrollPositionRestoration: 'top',
  anchorScrolling: 'enabled',
};
const inMemoryScrollingFeature: InMemoryScrollingFeature =
  withInMemoryScrolling(scrollConfig);

export const appConfig: ApplicationConfig = {
  providers: [provideRouter(routes, inMemoryScrollingFeature)],
};
```

Chapter 15: The Cart Item Card Component

15.1 Create It

Execute the command

```
ng g c
pages/cart/components/cart-item-card
```

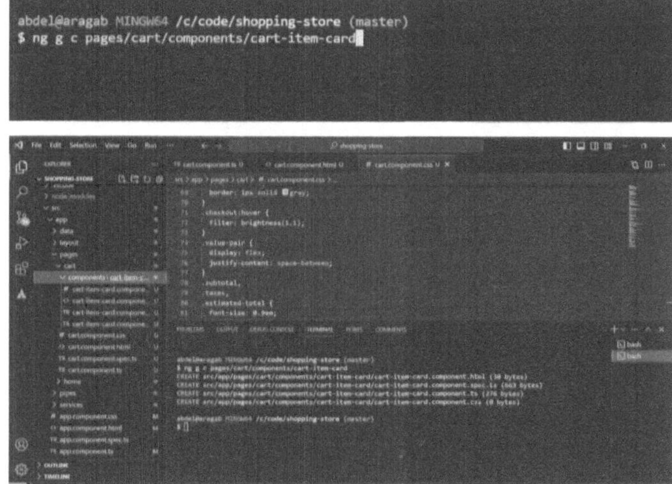

15.2 TS

It accepts the item as input and outputs the removal and quantity update events

```typescript
import { Component, EventEmitter, Input,
Output } from '@angular/core';
import { CartItem } from
'../../../../services/cart.service';

@Component({
  selector: 'app-cart-item-card',
  standalone: true,
  imports: [],
  templateUrl:
'./cart-item-card.component.html',
  styleUrl:
'./cart-item-card.component.css',
})
export class CartItemCardComponent {
  @Input() item!: CartItem;
  @Output() itemQuantityUpdate = new
EventEmitter<number>();
  @Output() removeItem = new
EventEmitter<void>();
  onQuantityChange(quantity: number) {

this.itemQuantityUpdate.next(quantity);
  }

  onRemoveItem() {
    this.removeItem.next();
  }
}
```

15.3 HTML

```
@if (item) {
<div class="wrapper">
  <div class="item">
    <img [src]="item.imageUrl"
[alt]="item.name" class="image" />
    <div class="name">
      {{ item.name }}
      <div class="detail">
        Free 90-day returns<br />
        Gift Eligible<br />
      </div>
    </div>
    <div class="price">
      <strong>${{ item.price }}</strong>
    </div>
  </div>
  <section class="controls">
    <span class="remove"
(click)="onRemoveItem()">Remove</span>
    <h4>Quantity Stepper</h4>
  </section>
</div>
}
```

```
 1  @if (item) {
 2  <div class="wrapper">
 3    <div class="item">
 4      <img [src]="item.imageUrl" [alt]="item.name" class="image" />
 5      <div class="name">
 6        {{ item.name }}
 7        <div class="detail">
 8          Free 90-day returns<br />
 9          Gift Eligible<br />
10        </div>
11      </div>
12      <div class="price">
13        <strong>${{ item.price }}</strong>
14      </div>
15    </div>
16    <section class="controls">
17      <span class="remove" (click)="onRemoveItem()">Remove</span>
18      <h4>Quantity Stepper</h4>
19    </section>
20  </div>
21  }
```

15.4 CSS

```
.wrapper {
  position: relative;
  width: 100%;
  height: 100%;
  padding: 40px 0px;
  border-top: 1px solid rgba(128, 128,
128, 0.2);
}
.item {
  width: 100%;
  display: grid;
  grid-template-columns: 100px auto
60px;
  cursor: default;
}
.image {
  width: 100px;
```

```css
    height: 100%;
    object-fit: contain;
  }
  .name {
    line-height: 1.6em;
    @media (min-width: 760px) {
      padding-right: 80px;
    }
  }
  .detail {
    opacity: 0.8;
    font-size: 0.8em;
    padding-top: 10px;
    line-height: 1.6em;
    display: none;
    @media (min-width: 760px) {
      display: block;
    }
  }
  .controls {
    display: flex;
    gap: 20px;
    align-items: center;
    position: absolute;
    right: 0px;
    padding-top: 20px;
    @media (min-width: 760px) {
      padding-top: 0px;
    }
  }
  .remove {
```

```
  text-decoration: underline;
  transform: scale(0.9);
  font-weight: 300;
  cursor: pointer;
}
```

```
 1  .wrapper {
 2    position: relative;
 3    width: 100%;
 4    height: 100%;
 5    padding: 40px 0px;
 6    border-top: 1px solid rgba(128, 128, 128, 0.2);
 7  }
 8  .item {
 9    width: 100%;
10    display: grid;
11    grid-template-columns: 100px auto 60px;
12    cursor: default;
13  }
14  .image {
15    width: 100px;
16    height: 100%;
17    object-fit: contain;
18  }
19  .name {
20    line-height: 1.6em;
21    @media (min-width: 760px) {
22      padding-right: 80px;
23    }
24  }
25  .detail {
26    opacity: 0.8;
27    font-size: 0.8em;
28    padding-top: 10px;
29    line-height: 1.6em;
30    display: none;
31    @media (min-width: 760px) {
32      display: block;
33    }
34  }
35  .controls {
36    display: flex;
37    gap: 20px;
38    align-items: center;
39    position: absolute;
40    right: 0px;
41    padding-top: 20px;
42    @media (min-width: 760px) {
43      padding-top: 0px;
44    }
45  }
46  .remove {
47    text-decoration: underline;
48    transform: scale(0.9);
49    font-weight: 300;
50    cursor: pointer;
51  }
```

15.5 Use It

Import it in the CartComponent as follows

```typescript
import { Component, computed } from
'@angular/core';
import { CartService } from
'../../services/cart.service';
import { CartItemCardComponent } from
'./components/cart-item-card/cart-item-c
ard.component';

@Component({
  selector: 'app-cart',
  standalone: true,
  imports: [CartItemCardComponent],
  templateUrl: './cart.component.html',
  styleUrl: './cart.component.css',
})
export class CartComponent {
  count = computed(() =>
this.cartService.cart().count);
  total = computed(() =>
this.cartService.cart().total);
  items = computed(() =>
this.cartService.cart().items);

  constructor(private cartService:
CartService) {}
}
```

```typescript
import { Component, computed } from '@angular/core';
import { CartService } from '../../services/cart.service';
import { CartItemCardComponent } from './components/cart-item-card/cart-item-card.component';

@Component({
  selector: 'app-cart',
  standalone: true,
  imports: [CartItemCardComponent],
  templateUrl: './cart.component.html',
  styleUrl: './cart.component.css',
})
export class CartComponent {
  count = computed(() => this.cartService.cart().count);
  total = computed(() => this.cartService.cart().total);
  items = computed(() => this.cartService.cart().items);

  constructor(private cartService: CartService) {}
}
```

Declare onItemQuantityUpdate and onRemoveItem methods as follows

```typescript
  onItemQuantityUpdate(quantity: number, id: string) {
    let increase = true;
    const item = this.items().find((t) => t.id === id);
    if (quantity < item!.quantity) increase = false;
    if (increase) {

this.cartService.increaseItem(item!);
    } else {

this.cartService.decreaseItem(item!);
    }
  }

  onRemoveItem(id: string) {
    const item = this.items().find((t) => t.id === id);
    this.cartService.removeItem(item!);
```

```
  }
```

```
19  onItemQuantityUpdate(quantity: number, id: string) {
20    let increase = true;
21    const item = this.items().find((t) => t.id === id);
22    if (quantity < item!.quantity) increase = false;
23    if (increase) {
24      this.cartService.increaseItem(item!);
25    } else {
26      this.cartService.decreaseItem(item!);
27    }
28  }
29
30  onRemoveItem(id: string) {
31    const item = this.items().find((t) => t.id === id);
32    this.cartService.removeItem(item!);
33  }
```

Now, replace the item name in the for loop by the cart-item-card as follows
Replace this

```
<h3>{{ item.name }}</h3>
```

by this

```
<app-cart-item-card
    [item]="item"

    (itemQuantityUpdate)="onItemQuantityUpdate($event, item.id)"

    (removeItem)="onRemoveItem(item.id)"
    ></app-cart-item-card>
```

```
15    <div class="arrival">
16      <strong>Arrives by Wed, Jan 24</strong>
17    </div>
18    <div class="content">
19      @for (item of items(); track item.id) {
20      <app-cart-item-card
21        [item]="item"
22        (itemQuantityUpdate)="onItemQuantityUpdate($event, item.id)"
23        (removeItem)="onRemoveItem(item.id)"
24        ></app-cart-item-card>
25      }
26    </div>
27  </div>
```

Start the application, add some products and go to the shopping cart page. It should look like this

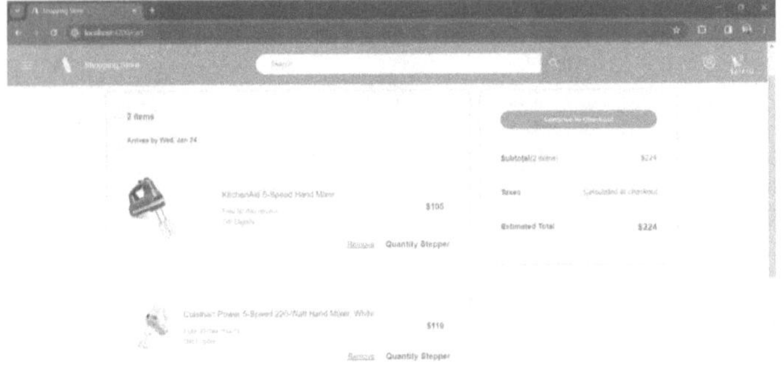

Chapter 16: Quantity Stepper

16.1 Create It

Execute the command

```
ng g c
pages/cart/components/quantity-stepper
```

16.2 TS

```ts
import { Component, EventEmitter, Input,
Output } from '@angular/core';

@Component({
  selector: 'app-quantity-stepper',
  standalone: true,
```

```typescript
  imports: [],
  templateUrl:
'./quantity-stepper.component.html',
  styleUrl:
'./quantity-stepper.component.css',
})
export class QuantityStepperComponent {
  @Input() quantity: number = 1;
  @Output() quantityChange = new
EventEmitter<number>();

  onIncreaseQuantity() {

this.quantityChange.next(this.quantity +
1);
  }

  onDecreaseQuantity() {
    if (this.quantity > 1)
this.quantityChange.next(this.quantity -
1);
  }
}
```

```typescript
import { Component, EventEmitter, Input, Output } from '@angular/core';

@Component({
  selector: 'app-quantity-stepper',
  standalone: true,
  imports: [],
  templateUrl: './quantity-stepper.component.html',
  styleUrl: './quantity-stepper.component.css',
})
export class QuantityStepperComponent {
  @Input() quantity: number = 1;
  @Output() quantityChange = new EventEmitter<number>();

  onIncreaseQuantity() {
    this.quantityChange.next(this.quantity + 1);
  }

  onDecreaseQuantity() {
    if (this.quantity > 1) this.quantityChange.next(this.quantity - 1);
  }
}
```

16.3 HTML

```html
<div class="wrapper">
  <div class="button" (click)="onDecreaseQuantity()">-</div>
  <div class="quantity">
    <strong>{{ quantity }}</strong>
  </div>
  <div class="button" (click)="onIncreaseQuantity()">+</div>
</div>
```

16.4 CSS

```css
.wrapper {
  width: 140px;
```

```css
  height: 34px;
  display: grid;
  grid-template-columns: 25px 70px 25px;
  border: 1px solid rgba(128, 128, 128,
0.3);
  border-radius: 30px;
  place-content: center center;
  place-items: center center;
  padding: 0px 40px;
  user-select: none;
}
.button {
  width: 25px;
  font-weight: 200;
  font-size: 20px;
  display: flex;
  justify-content: center;
  align-items: center;
  cursor: pointer;
}
.button:hover {
  color: #ffffff;
  background-color: gray;
  border-radius: 50%;
}
```

```css
1   .wrapper {
2     width: 140px;
3     height: 34px;
4     display: grid;
5     grid-template-columns: 25px 70px 25px;
6     border: 1px solid rgba(128, 128, 128, 0.3);
7     border-radius: 30px;
8     place-content: center center;
9     place-items: center center;
10    padding: 0px 40px;
11    user-select: none;
12  }
13  .button {
14    width: 25px;
15    font-weight: 200;
16    font-size: 20px;
17    display: flex;
18    justify-content: center;
19    align-items: center;
20    cursor: pointer;
21  }
22  .button:hover {
23    color: #ffffff;
24    background-color: gray;
25    border-radius: 50%;
26  }
```

16.5 Use It

Import it in the CartItemCardComponent as follows

```typescript
import { Component, EventEmitter, Input, Output } from '@angular/core';
import { CartItem } from '../../../../services/cart.service';
import { QuantityStepperComponent } from '../quantity-stepper/quantity-stepper.component';

@Component({
  selector: 'app-cart-item-card',
  standalone: true,
  imports: [QuantityStepperComponent],
```

```
  templateUrl:
'./cart-item-card.component.html',
  styleUrl:
'./cart-item-card.component.css',
})
export class CartItemCardComponent {
  ...
}
```

```typescript
1   import { Component, EventEmitter, Input, Output } from '@angular/core';
2   import { CartItem } from '../../../../services/cart.service';
3   import { QuantityStepperComponent } from '../quantity-stepper/quantity-stepper.component';
4
5   @Component({
6     selector: 'app-cart-item-card',
7     standalone: true,
8     imports: [QuantityStepperComponent],
9     templateUrl: './cart-item-card.component.html',
10    styleUrl: './cart-item-card.component.css',
11  })
12  export class CartItemCardComponent {
13
```

In the cart-item-card.component.html replace the placeholder

```html
    <h4>Quantity Stepper</h4>
```

by the component tag

```html
    <app-quantity-stepper
      [quantity]="item.quantity"

(quantityChange)="onQuantityChange($event)"
      ></app-quantity-stepper>
```

Start the application, add some items to the shopping cart and try to use the quantity stepper

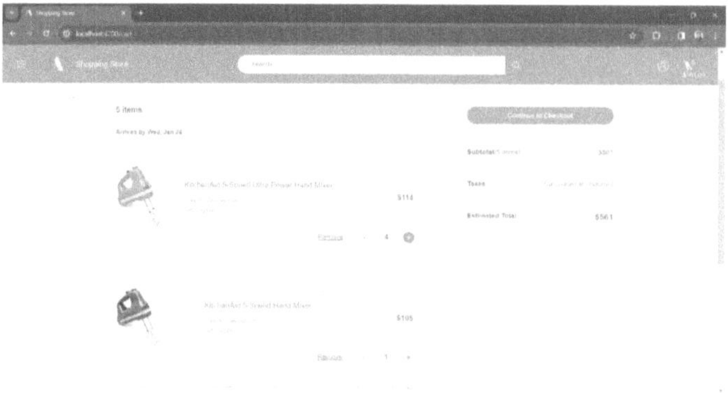

Shopping Store
Search

5 items

Arrives by Wed, Jan 24

Continue to Checkout

Subtotal (5 items)

Taxes

Estimated Total $561

KitchenAid 5-Speed Ultra Power Hand Mixer
$114

Remove   4

KitchenAid 5-Speed Hand Mixer
$105

Remove   1

Chapter 17: The Node.js Application

17.1 Create The Application

Create a new folder "node-shopping-store", navigate within the folder and execute the command
`npm init`

```
Microsoft Windows [Version 10.0.22621.3085]
(c) Microsoft Corporation. All rights reserved.

C:\code\node-shopping-store>npm init
```

```
C:\Windows\System32\cmd.e  ×   +  ∨                                  —   □   ×

Use 'npm install <pkg>' afterwards to install a package and
save it as a dependency in the package.json file.

Press ^C at any time to quit.
package name: (shopping-store) node-shopping-store
version: (1.0.0)
description:
entry point: (index.js)
test command:
git repository:
keywords:
author:
license: (ISC)
About to write to C:\code\node-shopping-store\package.json:

{
  "name": "node-shopping-store",
  "version": "1.0.0",
  "description": "",
  "main": "index.js",
  "scripts": {
    "test": "echo \"Error: no test specified\" && exit 1"
  },
  "author": "",
  "license": "ISC"
}


Is this OK? (yes)

C:\code\node-shopping-store>
```

Open the project in Visual Studio Code

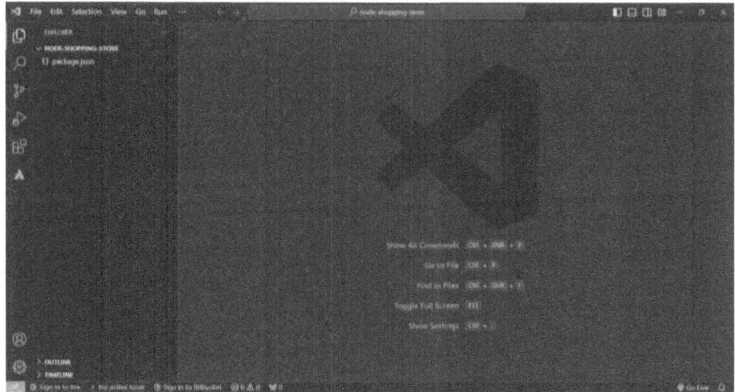

17.2 Install the Dependencies

We will install the following dependencies:
- cors: because I will make requests to the Stripe server.
- express: to create the backend server.
- stripe: to access the Stripe API from our server.
- dotenv: to manage environment variables and store our secret keys.
- nodemon: automatically restarts the Node.js application when detect changes.

Open terminal and execute the command

```
npm i cors express stripe dotenv nodemon
```

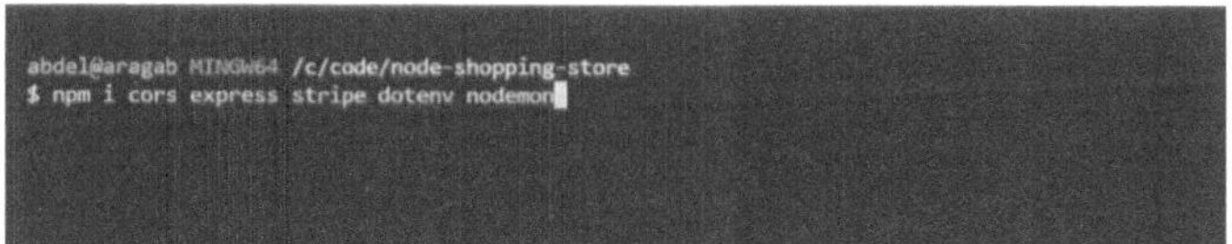

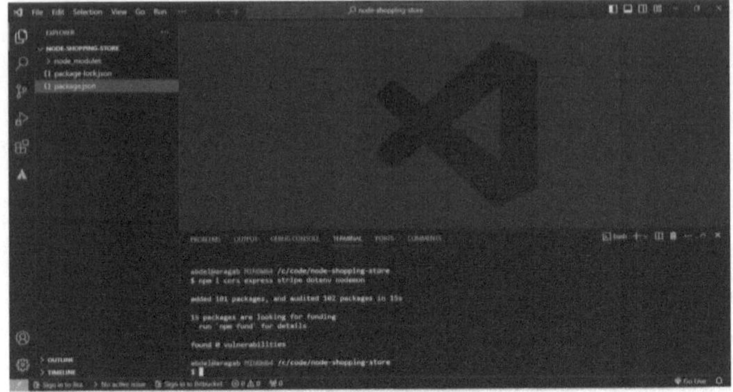

Add this script to the scripts object in the package.json

```
"start": "nodemon index.js"
```

Create a .env file and paste your Stripe Secret Key as follows

```
STRIPE_SECRET_KEY=sk_123456666...
```

17.3 Create the Server

Create a new index.js file and write the code of the
server

```
const cors = require("cors");
const express = require("express");
require("dotenv").config();

const stripe =
require("stripe")(process.env.STRIPE_SEC
RET_KEY);

const app = express();

app.use(express.json());
app.use(cors());

// Routes
app.get("/", (req, res) => {
  res.send("Server is running..");
});

app.listen(8000, () => {
  console.log("Server started at port
8000");
});
```

```javascript
1   const cors = require("cors");
2   const express = require("express");
3   require("dotenv").config();
4
5   const stripe = require("stripe")(process.env.STRIPE_SECRET_KEY);
6
7   const app = express();
8
9   app.use(express.json());
10  app.use(cors());
11
12  // Routes
13  app.get("/", (req, res) => {
14    res.send("Server is running..");
15  });
16
17  app.listen(8000, () => {
18    console.log("Server started at port 8000");
19  });
```

To start the application, open the terminal and execute
the command

```
npm start
```

```
abdel@aragab MINGW64 /c/code/node-shopping-store
$ npm start
```

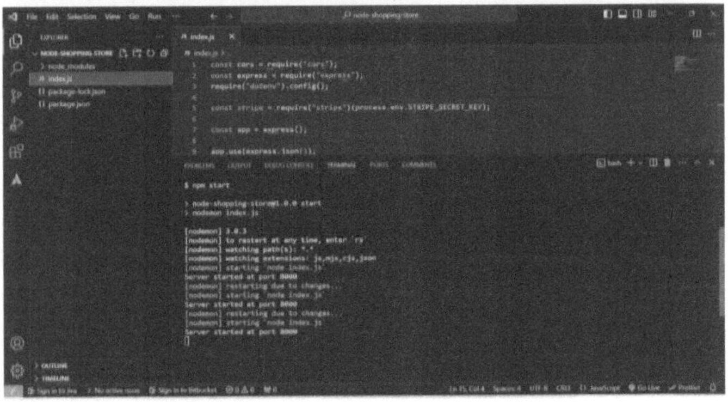

Open the browser and navigate to http://localhost:8000/

A white page with the message "Server is running..."
should be displayed

17.4 Charge the Customer

Now I will create a post route to charge the customer. It
will be called via the frontend.
Add it to index.js under the get route.

```
app.post("/api/create-checkout-session",
async (req, res) => {
  const origin = req.get("origin");
  const lineItems = req.body.map((item)
=> ({
    price_data: {
      currency: "usd",
      product_data: {
        name: item.name,
        images: [item.imageUrl],
      },
      unit_amount: Math.round(item.price
* 100),
    },
    quantity: item.quantity,
  }));
```

```
const session = await
stripe.checkout.sessions.create({
    payment_method_types: ["card"],
    line_items: lineItems,
    mode: "payment",
    success_url: origin + "/success",
    cancel_url: origin + "/cancel",
  });

  res.json({ id: session.id });
});
```

```javascript
17  app.post("/api/create-checkout-session", async (req, res) => {
18    const origin = req.get("origin");
19    const lineItems = req.body.map((item) => ({
20      price_data: {
21        currency: "usd",
22        product_data: {
23          name: item.name,
24          images: [item.imageUrl],
25        },
26        unit_amount: Math.round(item.price * 100),
27      },
28      quantity: item.quantity,
29    }));
30
31    const session = await stripe.checkout.sessions.create({
32      payment_method_types: ["card"],
33      line_items: lineItems,
34      mode: "payment",
35      success_url: origin + "/success",
36      cancel_url: origin + "/cancel",
37    });
38
39    res.json({ id: session.id });
40  });
```

Now that the server is ready, we can continue working
on the Angular app.

Chapter 18: Checkout

18.1 Install the Stripe Dependency

Let's install the Stripe dependency for our Angular
application
Execute the command

```
npm i @stripe/stripe-js
```

```
abdel@aragab MINGW64 /c/code/shopping-store (master)
$ npm i @stripe/stripe-js
```

18.2 Generate the Environments

I will use the environment to save our stripe keys. To
generate the environments
To create the environments, execute the command

```
ng g environments
```

```
abdel@aragab MINGW64 /c/code/shopping-store (master)
$ ng g environments
```

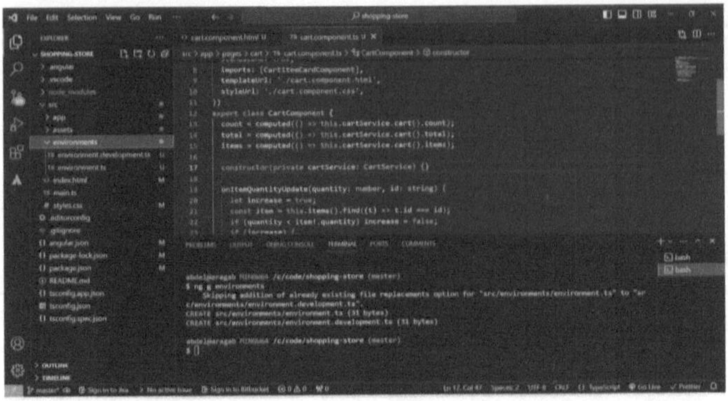

Add your Stripe public key to the environments as follows

```
export const environment = {
  STRIPE_PK:
'pk_1234567890ABCDEFGHIJKLMNOP...',
};
```

```
1  export const environment = {
2    STRIPE_PK: 'pk_1234567890ABCDEFGHIJKLMNOP...',
3  };
```

18.3 Provide the HttpClientModule

Add the `HttpClientModule` to the provider array in **app.config.ts** as follows

```
import { ApplicationConfig,
importProvidersFrom } from
'@angular/core';
import {
  InMemoryScrollingFeature,
  InMemoryScrollingOptions,
```

```typescript
  provideRouter,
  withInMemoryScrolling,
} from '@angular/router';

import { routes } from './app.routes';
import { HttpClientModule } from
'@angular/common/http';

const scrollConfig:
InMemoryScrollingOptions = {
  scrollPositionRestoration: 'top',
  anchorScrolling: 'enabled',
};
const inMemoryScrollingFeature:
InMemoryScrollingFeature =
  withInMemoryScrolling(scrollConfig);

export const appConfig:
ApplicationConfig = {
  providers: [
    provideRouter(routes,
inMemoryScrollingFeature),

importProvidersFrom(HttpClientModule),
  ],
};
```

```typescript
import { ApplicationConfig, importProvidersFrom } from '@angular/core';
import {
  InMemoryScrollingFeature,
  InMemoryScrollingOptions,
  provideRouter,
  withInMemoryScrolling,
} from '@angular/router';

import { routes } from './app.routes';
import { HttpClientModule } from '@angular/common/http';

const scrollConfig: InMemoryScrollingOptions = {
  scrollPositionRestoration: 'top',
  anchorScrolling: 'enabled',
};
const inMemoryScrollingFeature: InMemoryScrollingFeature =
  withInMemoryScrolling(scrollConfig);

export const appConfig: ApplicationConfig = {
  providers: [
    provideRouter(routes, inMemoryScrollingFeature),
    importProvidersFrom(HttpClientModule),
  ],
};
```

18.4 Update the Cart Component

Inject the `HttpClient` into the constructor as follows
```
constructor(private cartService:
CartService, private http: HttpClient) {}
```

```
constructor(private cartService: CartService, private http: HttpClient) {}
```

Declare the onCheckout method as follows
```
async onCheckout() {
    const stripe = await
loadStripe(environment.STRIPE_PK);
    const body =
this.cartService.cart().items;
    const headers = {
      'Content-Type':
'application/json',
    };
```

```javascript
this.http

  .post('http://localhost:8000/api/create-checkout-session', body, {
    headers: headers,
  })
    .subscribe({
      next: async (response) => {
        const session = response as any;

        const result = await stripe?.redirectToCheckout({
          sessionId: session.id,
        });

        if (result?.error) {
          console.log(result?.error);
        }
      },
      error: (response) => {
        if (response?.error) {

console.log(response?.error);
        }
      },
    });
  }
```

```
38  async onCheckout() {
39    const stripe = await loadStripe(environment.STRIPE_PK);
40    const body = this.cartService.cart().items;
41    const headers = {
42      'Content-Type': 'application/json',
43    };
44
45    this.http
46      .post('http://localhost:8000/api/create-checkout-session', body, {
47        headers: headers,
48      })
49      .subscribe({
50        next: async (response) => {
51          const session = response as any;
52
53          const result = await stripe?.redirectToCheckout({
54            sessionId: session.id,
55          });
56
57          if (result?.error) {
58            console.log(result?.error);
59          }
60        },
61        error: (response) => {
62          if (response?.error) {
63            console.log(response?.error);
64          }
65        },
66      });
67  }
```

Update the cart.component.html to add the click handler for the checkout button

```
<button class="checkout"
(click)="onCheckout()">
    <strong>Continue to
Checkout</strong>
    </button>
```

```
29  <button class="checkout" (click)="onCheckout()">
30    <strong>Continue to Checkout</strong>
31  </button>
```

Start the application, add products and proceed to checkout

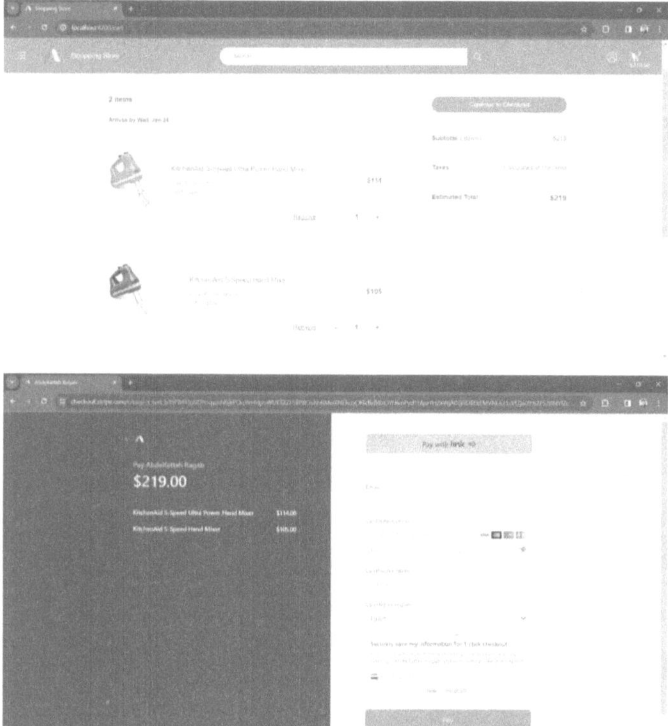

Congratulations! You have successfully integrated Stripe into your shopping store and can process payments from your clients online successfully.

For the sake of completeness, I will create two more pages to show the result of the payment processing, one for success and one for abandonment.

Chapter 19: The Success Page

19.1 Create It

Execute the command

```
ng g c pages/success
```

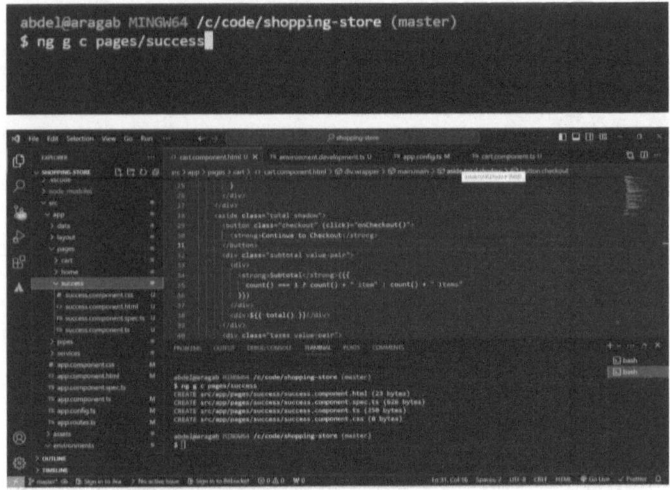

19.2 Add Route

Add a new route for the success page in the app.route.ts as follows

```
import { Routes } from
'@angular/router';
```

```
import { HomeComponent } from
'./pages/home/home.component';
import { CartComponent } from
'./pages/cart/cart.component';
import { SuccessComponent } from
'./pages/success/success.component';

export const routes: Routes = [
  { path: '', redirectTo: 'home',
pathMatch: 'full' },
  { path: 'home', component:
HomeComponent },
  { path: 'cart', component:
CartComponent },
  { path: 'success', component:
SuccessComponent },
];
```

```
1   import { Routes } from '@angular/router';
2   import { HomeComponent } from './pages/home/home.component';
3   import { CartComponent } from './pages/cart/cart.component';
4   import { SuccessComponent } from './pages/success/success.component';
5
6   export const routes: Routes = [
7     { path: '', redirectTo: 'home', pathMatch: 'full' },
8     { path: 'home', component: HomeComponent },
9     { path: 'cart', component: CartComponent },
10    { path: 'success', component: SuccessComponent },
11  ];
```

19.3 TS

```
import { Component } from
'@angular/core';

@Component({
```

```
  selector: 'app-success',
  standalone: true,
  imports: [],
  templateUrl:
'./success.component.html',
  styleUrl: './success.component.css',
})
export class SuccessComponent {}
```

```
 1   import { Component } from '@angular/core';
 2
 3   @Component({{
 4     selector: 'app-success',
 5     standalone: true,
 6     imports: [],
 7     templateUrl: './success.component.html',
 8     styleUrl: './success.component.css',
 9   })
10   export class SuccessComponent {}
```

19.4 HTML

```
<div class="wrapper">
  <img class="image"
src="assets/icons/success.png" />
  <h1>Congratulations!</h1>
  <p class="text">Thank you! Your
payment has been received.</p>
</div>
```

```
 1   <div class="wrapper">
 2     <img class="image" src="assets/icons/success.png" />
 3     <h1>Congratulations!</h1>
 4     <p class="text">Thank you! Your payment has been received.</p>
 5   </div>
```

19.5 CSS

```css
.wrapper {
  display: flex;
  flex-direction: column;
  justify-content: center;
  align-items: center;
  padding: 100px;
  gap: 20px;
  cursor: default;
  text-align: center;
}
.image {
  width: 100px;
  height: 100%;
  object-fit: contain;
}
.text {
  font-size: 1.2em;
}
```

```css
1   .wrapper {
2     display: flex;
3     flex-direction: column;
4     justify-content: center;
5     align-items: center;
6     padding: 100px;
7     gap: 20px;
8     cursor: default;
9     text-align: center;
10  }
11  .image {
12    width: 100px;
13    height: 100%;
14    object-fit: contain;
15  }
16  .text {
17    font-size: 1.2em;
18  }
```

19.6 Use It

Stripe redirects you to the success page after successful payment. We have set this up in the node.js checkout method.

You can visit any page at any time by entering its path in the address bar.
http://localhost:4200/success

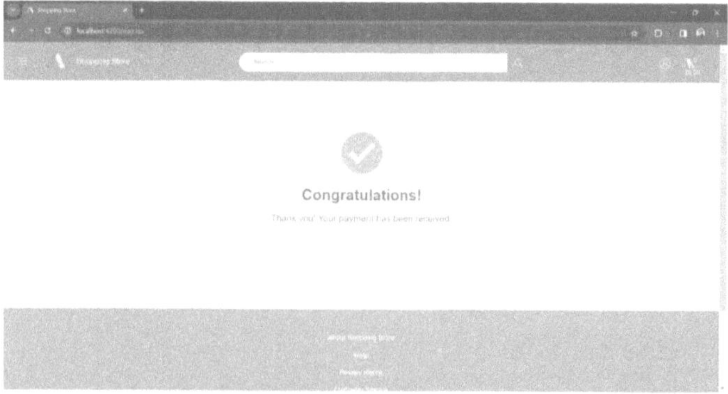

For a good user experience, I will add a button that redirects the user back to the home page so they can continue shopping.

Chapter 20: The Continue Shopping Button

20.1 Create It

Execute the command

```
ng g c
pages/home/components/btn-continue
```

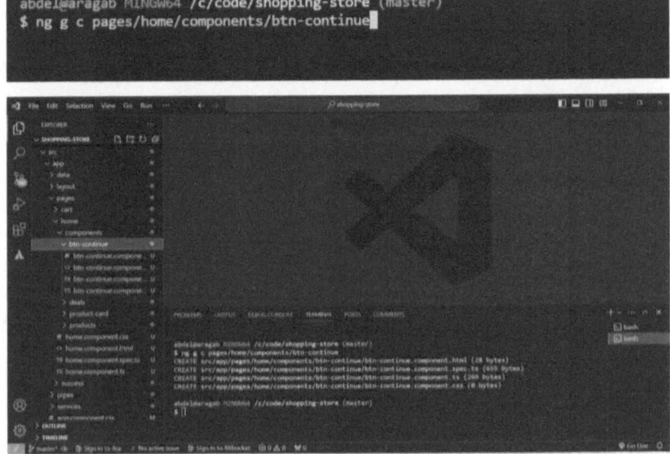

20.2 TS

Import the RouterLink

```
import { Component } from
'@angular/core';
```

```
import { RouterLink } from
'@angular/router';

@Component({
  selector: 'app-btn-continue',
  standalone: true,
  imports: [RouterLink],
  templateUrl:
'./btn-continue.component.html',
  styleUrl:
'./btn-continue.component.css',
})
export class BtnContinueComponent {}
```

```
 1  import { Component } from '@angular/core';
 2  import { RouterLink } from '@angular/router';
 3
 4  @Component({
 5    selector: 'app-btn-continue',
 6    standalone: true,
 7    imports: [RouterLink],
 8    templateUrl: './btn-continue.component.html',
 9    styleUrl: './btn-continue.component.css',
10  })
11  export class BtnContinueComponent {}
```

20.3 HTML

```
<div class="btn" routerLink="/">Continue
Shopping</div>
```

```
 1  <div class="btn" routerLink="/">Continue Shopping</div>
```

20.4 CSS

```
.btn {
  margin-top: 50px;
```

```css
    width: 100%;
    color: #ffffff;
    background-color: var(--accent-color);
    height: 36px;
    border-radius: 30px;
    cursor: pointer;
    outline: none;
    border: 1px solid gray;
    padding: 0px 20px;
    display: flex;
    justify-content: center;
    align-items: center;
}
.btn:hover {
    filter: brightness(1.1);
}
```

```css
1   .btn {
2     margin-top: 50px;
3     width: 100%;
4     color: #ffffff;
5     background-color: var(--accent-color);
6     height: 36px;
7     border-radius: 30px;
8     cursor: pointer;
9     outline: none;
10    border: 1px solid gray;
11    padding: 0px 20px;
12    display: flex;
13    justify-content: center;
14    align-items: center;
15  }
16  .btn:hover {
17    filter: brightness(1.1);
18  }
```

20.5 Use It

Import it in the SuccessComponent as follows

```
import { Component } from
'@angular/core';
import { BtnContinueComponent } from
'../home/components/btn-continue/btn-con
tinue.component';

@Component({
  selector: 'app-success',
  standalone: true,
  imports: [BtnContinueComponent],
  templateUrl:
'./success.component.html',
  styleUrl: './success.component.css',
})
export class SuccessComponent {}
```

```
1   import { Component } from '@angular/core';
2   import { BtnContinueComponent } from '../home/components/btn-continue/btn-continue.component';
3
4   @Component({
5     selector: 'app-success',
6     standalone: true,
7     imports: [BtnContinueComponent],
8     templateUrl: './success.component.html',
9     styleUrl: './success.component.css',
10  })
11  export class SuccessComponent {}
```

In the success.component.html, insert it at the end as follows

```
<div class="wrapper">
  <img class="image"
src="assets/icons/success.png" />
  <h1>Congratulations!</h1>
```

```
<p class="text">Thank you! Your
payment has been received.</p>
  <app-btn-continue></app-btn-continue>
</div>
```

```
1  <div class="wrapper">
2    <img class="image" src="assets/icons/success.png" />
3    <h1>Congratulations!</h1>
4    <p class="text">Thank you! Your payment has been received.</p>
5    <app-btn-continue></app-btn-continue>
6  </div>
7
```

Open the success page in your browser now

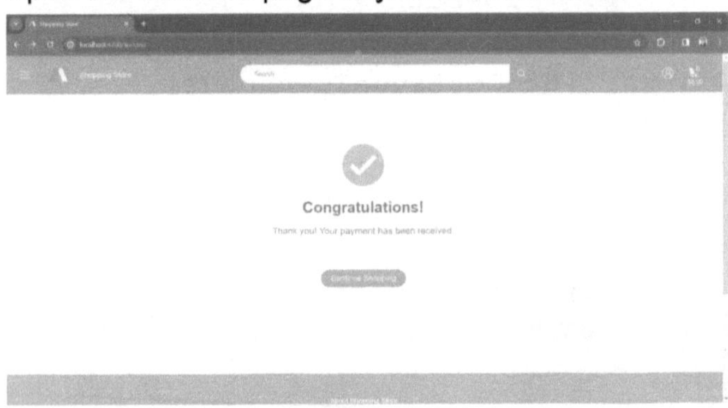

Chapter 21. The Cancel Page

21.1 Create It

Execute the command

```
ng g c pages/cancel
```

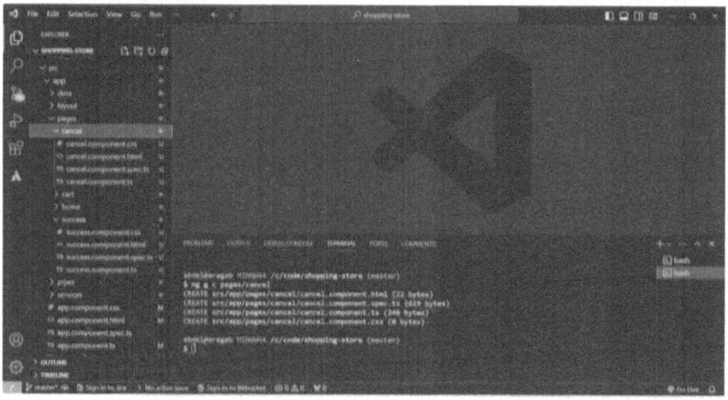

21.2 Add Route

Add a new route for the cancel page in the app.route.ts
as follows

```
import { Routes } from
'@angular/router';
import { HomeComponent } from
'./pages/home/home.component';
import { CartComponent } from
'./pages/cart/cart.component';
```

```typescript
import { SuccessComponent } from
'./pages/success/success.component';
import { CancelComponent } from
'./pages/cancel/cancel.component';

export const routes: Routes = [
  { path: '', redirectTo: 'home',
pathMatch: 'full' },
  { path: 'home', component:
HomeComponent },
  { path: 'cart', component:
CartComponent },
  { path: 'success', component:
SuccessComponent },
  { path: 'cancel', component:
CancelComponent },
];
```

```typescript
1   import { Routes } from '@angular/router';
2   import { HomeComponent } from './pages/home/home.component';
3   import { CartComponent } from './pages/cart/cart.component';
4   import { SuccessComponent } from './pages/success/success.component';
5   import { CancelComponent } from './pages/cancel/cancel.component';
6
7   export const routes: Routes = [
8     { path: '', redirectTo: 'home', pathMatch: 'full' },
9     { path: 'home', component: HomeComponent },
10    { path: 'cart', component: CartComponent },
11    { path: 'success', component: SuccessComponent },
12    { path: 'cancel', component: CancelComponent },
13  ];
```

21.3 TS

Import the BtnContinueComponent, as we will also use
it here

```typescript
import { Component } from
'@angular/core';
```

```typescript
import { BtnContinueComponent } from
'../home/components/btn-continue/btn-con
tinue.component';

@Component({
  selector: 'app-cancel',
  standalone: true,
  imports: [BtnContinueComponent],
  templateUrl:
'./cancel.component.html',
  styleUrl: './cancel.component.css',
})
export class CancelComponent {}
```

```typescript
import { Component } from '@angular/core';
import { BtnContinueComponent } from '../home/components/btn-continue/btn-continue.component';

@Component({
  selector: 'app-cancel',
  standalone: true,
  imports: [BtnContinueComponent],
  templateUrl: './cancel.component.html',
  styleUrl: './cancel.component.css',
})
export class CancelComponent {}
```

21.4 HTML

```html
<div class="wrapper">
  <img class="image"
src="assets/icons/cancel.png" />
  <h1>Cancelled!</h1>
  <p class="text">Your payment has been
cancelled.</p>
  <app-btn-continue></app-btn-continue>
</div>
```

```html
1  <div class="wrapper">
2    <img class="image" src="assets/icons/cancel.png" />
3    <h1>Cancelled!</h1>
4    <p class="text">Your payment has been cancelled.</p>
5    <app-btn-continue></app-btn-continue>
6  </div>
7
```

21.5 CSS

```css
.wrapper {
  display: flex;
  flex-direction: column;
  justify-content: center;
  align-items: center;
  padding: 100px;
  gap: 20px;
  cursor: default;
  text-align: center;
}
.image {
  width: 100px;
  height: 100%;
  object-fit: contain;
}
.text {
  font-size: 1.2em;
}
```

```css
.wrapper {
  display: flex;
  flex-direction: column;
  justify-content: center;
  align-items: center;
  padding: 100px;
  gap: 20px;
  cursor: default;
  text-align: center;
}
.image {
  width: 100px;
  height: 100%;
  object-fit: contain;
}
.text {
  font-size: 1.2em;
}
```

20.6 Use It

We have already set up Stripe so that it forwards to the reversal path in the event of an aborted payment.

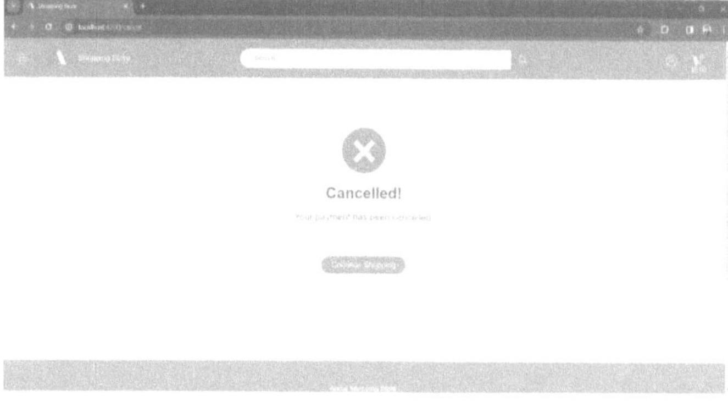

Conclusion

Congratulations on taking the first step towards a real business. Once you have completed this project, you can now move on to more advanced projects and move to full-stack development to have control over all parts of your application.
When you're ready, you can read my books on full-stack development, where I develop real applications for real businesses.
I am sure they are interesting and will answer all your questions.
Good luck!

—Abdelfattah Ragab

Don't miss out!

Receive an email when Abdelfattah Ragab publishes a new book. It's free and without obligation.

Also by Abdelfattah Ragab

- Shippo Integration in Angular
- Responsive Layouts: Flex, Grid and Multi-Column
- Angular HTTP
- Angular Reactive Forms

About the Author

Abdelfattah Ragab is a professional software developer with more than 20 years of experience.
https://abdelfattah-ragab.com

About the Publisher

Abdelfattah Ragab is a highly qualified and experienced software developer with over 20 years of experience in the industry. Specializing in front-end development, Abdelfattah Ragab has a deep understanding of Angular, JavaScript, TypeScript, HTML and CSS. Read more at https://abdelfattah-ragab.com